FIND YOUR PATH AND IMPROVE YOUR LIFE

BONNIE NILSSON

Published by Spines
ISBN: 979-8-89383-347-8

CONTENTS

Preface   7

 1. Who is Man? Who is a Woman?   9
 2. Who is God?   21
 3. He Knows You   29
 4. Many roads, only one way   43
 5. God's Creation   53
 6. Have you been tripped up in this life?   73
 7. Places of Worship   79
 8. When Heaven and Nature Sing   91
 9. Testimonies   97
10. The Final Chapter   101

Your Prayer of Salvation   111

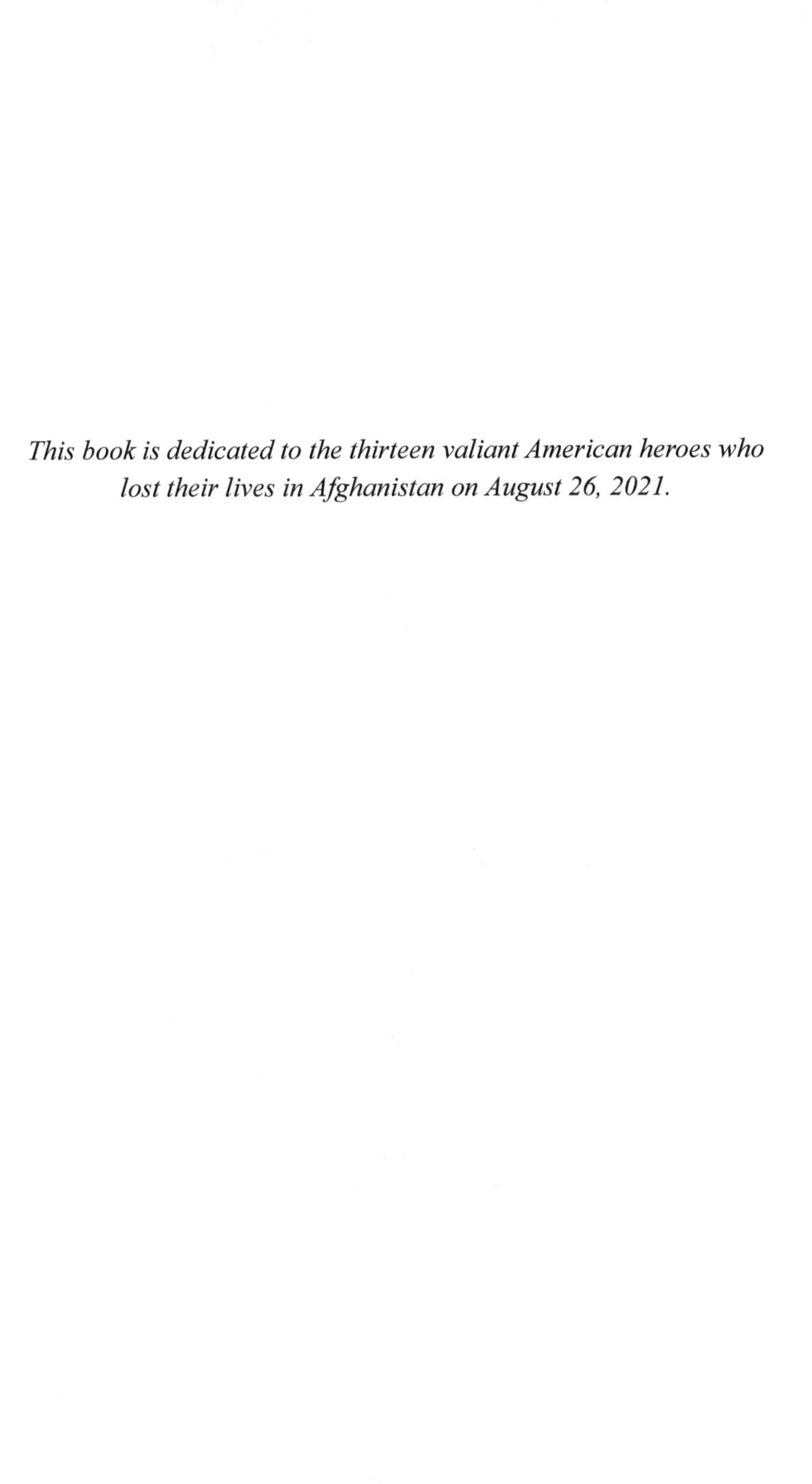

This book is dedicated to the thirteen valiant American heroes who lost their lives in Afghanistan on August 26, 2021.

California
Sgt. Nicole L. Gee
Cpl. Hunter Lopez
Lance Cpl. Dylan R. Merola
Lance Cpl. Kareem M. Nikoui

Indiana
Cpl. Humberto A. Sanchez

Massachusetts
Sgt. Johanny Rosario Pichardo

Missouri
Lance Cpl. Jared M. Schmitz

Nebraska
Cpl. Daegan W. Page

Ohio
Navy Corpsman Maxton W. Soviak

Tennessee
Staff Sgt. Ryan C. Knauss

Texas
Lance Cpl. David L. Espinoza

Utah
Staff Sgt. Darin T. Hoover

PREFACE

After my first book was published, I spoke to many people and started a YouTube channel to accompany the discussions on the spiritual man. As a nurse, I sought out and learned a great deal of knowledge about how to benefit the human body with simple practices and tweaks to the daily routine that improve it.

There is no sense in making physical changes and neglecting to care for the spiritual part of yourself. Cast your cares onto the Lord. With new insights into how much God loves you, you can reduce anxiety and stress and improve relationships. He truly loves you.

Regardless of what has happened to you in life or how you reacted, don't let emotions rule your life. You were created with a purpose. Your job is to find the path, and I promise to help you as best I can to get on that path that bears your name. That is my promise to you.

1

WHO IS MAN? WHO IS A WOMAN?

Man is inherently curious, driven by an insatiable thirst for understanding the world around them and their place within it. This curiosity has propelled humanity to explore the depths of the oceans, reach for the stars, and unravel the mysteries of the cosmos. Man is also a creature of empathy and compassion, capable of immense acts of kindness and solidarity, yet also prone to acts of cruelty and injustice. Through the lens of history, man emerges as both a builder and destroyer, shaping civilizations with feats of innovation and engineering while also grappling with the consequences of their actions on the planet and fellow beings. In essence, man is a multifaceted being, navigating the complexities of existence with a blend of intellect, emotion, and societal dynamics, constantly evolving and adapting in their quest for growth and fulfillment.

Womanhood is a narrative of perseverance and empowerment, echoing through generations of trailblazers who dared to dream and dare to act. It is a testament to the unwavering spirit that confronts adversity with resilience, transforms setbacks into opportunities, and inspires change through compassion and determination. Women stand as pillars of strength, nurturing families, communities, and societies with boundless compassion, wisdom, and moral clarity. In the tapestry of humanity, womanhood can be a determined force of nature, shaping destinies, and empowering ideals, goals, and outcomes.

To know who is man or who is woman we must first check the Scriptures. God formed man in His image took a rib from Adam and created a woman. Adam was the first father of humankind and Eve was the first mother.

I like the way the Message bible engages the first book of the bible the Book of Genesis as God speaks creation into being. On the sixth day God spoke the word, Let us make humans then in our image, make them reflect our image.

If you don't own a Message bible, don't worry! You can read the translation of The Book of Genesis online in the Message Bible. I hope you will find it awe-inspiring:

GREEK PHILOSOPHERS SOCRATES AND ARISTOTLE DESCRIBE HUMAN NATURE.

By definition, "human nature" includes the core characteristics (feelings, psychology, behaviors) shared by all people. We all have different experiences as humans in our lives, and this is where the disputes begin. Some people will tell you humans are 'good' or 'bad,' 'predators,' or 'capable of great kindness.' We can consider these terms people use by using what we know and what our culture and subcultures tell us. The group you are born into will pass on its particular ideas about what makes humans.

Human behavior is a varied topic. Feelings can change like the wind. That is the way our creator designed us. Yet, God has a grand plan for your existence. He did this through your soul (mind, will, and emotions), allowing you to communicate with the creator

God. How awesome is that? What must we do to communicate with God? How might we hear Him?

If you call out to Allah, will you hear a reply? Call out to Buddha in time of trouble, will he be there?

Reading God's word is an excellent place to start. The Word of God is living. He says in His word that many things will pass away. and His word is eternal. When you realize God's love for you, you will begin to understand His love for all people. You may dream more frequently, as I did. Your preference for some things will change. Your mind will start to change. You will acknowledge your part and may tell God you are sorry for past mistakes. You will get that new job. You will meet someone who also has decided to trust God. You will acknowledge that Jesus died on the cross for your sins. You may have dreams that show you the truth about an area of concern. You will ask God to be with you and to help you. As I did, you will begin to test the Spirits. There is God, Jesus, and the Holy Spirit. Satan is a fallen angel spirit, and he is a liar.

I tested the spirits using the words of the bible. Is there a biblical precedent for what I heard? After finding a scriptural source for what I thought I had understood, I would pray about it. I would ask God to show me the truth or fallacy of the message I received. Sometimes a few days would have passed to get the answer. You will want to be well-rested before you press into God for understanding.

You will learn that your words have real power.

You will learn the significance of the Ten Commandments.

As the Old Testament comes to a close, Haggai is the Prophet separated from the Prophet Zechariah by one hundred years. The exiles returned to the Holy City from captivity in Babylon in 536 BC. The first group of fifty thousand people were led back to a place called The Promised Land by Zerubbabel, a descendant of

David in the Royal House of David. The book of Haggai records the rebuilding of the Temple. The people's reluctance and unwillingness of the returned exiles and their fear of the Persian Government because they built without special permission (Ezra, Chps 4-16.)

In the second year of Darius, the Persian King resigned after 15 years following Cyrus, who commanded the building of the city with King Herod the Great with the laying of the foundation of the Temple and generally being credited with the completion of the project as the Temple was referred to as Herod's Temple. Biblical scholars believe Cyrus to be the son of Ester. (Ezra Chapter 1; Isa 45:13)

Yet, God's people were a sorry lot. Unbelief leaves God out every time. God asks the people to consider their ways. I suggest you read the book of Haggai and listen to God as he counsels his people and discusses his steps of correction, reminding them He has never left them.

The final Chapter of Malachi in the Old Testament is the last prophetic words the people of God would hear, representing 400 years of silence. While the Old Testament period closed and the time of the New Testament began, it was a hectic time. In many ways, that time mirrors our world in this present time. Seek Truth, and the greater your ability to discern what you hear, the greater you will find yourself seeking after Truth more significantly. There were many gods that the people worshipped. These gods were idols. Nowhere in the Bible does it tell us these gods intervened for the people who worshipped them.

I have talked to many believers who tell me the end times are near. I agree and ask them to tell me what exactly that means. They tell me it is the last days, evil abounds, and the Rapture is imminent.

I take a gut punch every time. Has anyone thought about the enormous work required to preach the Gospel to the ends of the earth? The new skills needed to Shepherd a worldwide flock and the boatloads of funds necessary to save roughly a billion souls globally before the Rapture. Has the Gospel been preached unto all the earth?

I think of the testimony of Bob Jones, a Christian man who was saved as he stood in a field one day. Bob's Spirit was taken to Heaven after having a heart attack and flat-lining. As He stood in line, he noticed he had a white robe on. As Bob approached, the Lord greeted him by name. It was not as seamless as Bob thought, and Jesus, rather than allowing him to pass through the gate to Heaven, the Lord asked Bob to look to his left.

Bob could hardly believe what he saw—a line of people as long as his eye could see, all in line for Hell. Some had buildings stuck all over them; others had jewels, money, gold golf clubs, cruise liners, and mansions. Bob knew these people had put these things as must-haves in their lives while none had thought of God. Bob felt terrible because when you love God, he gives you the desires of your heart, even if they are golf clubs.

Jesus said, "Bob, won't you go back and save these people from hell?'

And as the obedient man of God, Bob said, "Yes, Lord, I will."

If you have ever had the pleasure of sitting in the presence of Bob Jones, you no doubt remember his assured and matter-of-fact manner of speech. He looked at me one day and said, "Sweetheart, you can eat nuts." I was 47 years old at the time and had been allergic to nuts since the age of two. Because of the allergy, I visited more Emergency rooms than I could count.

In 2019, I was surfing the web and saw Bob Jones in a YouTube video. I jumped for joy to see this great man of God. He looked older, but his Spirit was as alive as ever. Anyone who knew Bob knew his assured manner of speech—God said, so you knew he was very close to God. I had been twelve years free of a nut allergy and the asthma that was somehow related to it.

I then remembered Oral Roberts passed in 2018, and after checking, I found Bob Jones passed on Valentine's Day 2013. Oh, you sweet souls in Heaven, please wait a season until we can get this mess cleared up in the body.

Your life will improve when you have a deeper relationship with God. If you desire to change your life, this is the only way to ensure lasting results because that is what happened to me. You have no idea how loving the Lord is to his children. Let the Lord out of the box you have put him in. Don't be mad at God for an event that may have rocked your world. God is Love, and Satan comes to seek, kill, and destroy.

I am sorry that when I first learned about Christ, some preachers who professed to love God were teaching false doctrine. Teaching that one can tithe their way to a new car. Tithe so we can make Jesus happy when he is sad. Say what? The Lord of Lords can be without our help. The Lord of Lords requires our belief, obedience, and love. He hung on the cross and shed His blood so we could partner with Him and not grow weary. God knows all things—the end from the beginning.

> For the word of God is alive and active. Sharper than any double-edged sword, it penetrates even to dividing soul and spirit, joints and marrow; it judges the thoughts and attitudes of the heart. NIV
>
> — HEBREWS 4:12

> And we all, with unveiled faces, beholding the glory of the Lord, are being transformed into the same image from one degree of

recognition to another. For this comes from the Lord, who is the Spirit.

— 2 CORINTHIANS 3;18

For behold, the day comes, that shall burn as an oven: and all the proud, yea and all those who do wickedly, shall be stubble; and the day that comes shall burn them up, saith the LORD of Hosts. That is, it shall leave them to wither and riot.

But unto You who fear my name shall the Son of righteousness arise with healing in His wings, and you shall grow up as stalls' calves.

— MALACHI CHAPTER FOUR 1-2

I know and have seen with my own eyes when released from the barn to the open meadow, young calves can be seen jumping for joy, twisting, and shaking every which way.

What's in your mouth?

The tongue with the lips and teeth allows you to speak.

Who so keepeth his mouth and tongue keepeth his soul from troubles.

— PROVERBS 21:23

But the tongue can no man tame; it is an unruly evil, full of deadly poison.

— JAMES 3;8

Keep your mouth shut if something deadly is likely to fly out. I have always been a talker. So, the first lesson was about the power

I had in my spoken words. God did not have to work on my dress or personal habits. I had returned from church, and I was getting a profound lesson on the power of words and the authority of the words I speak, more to the point.

I had a lovely back bedroom with a bay window, a sunny and bright room most days, even in winter. It was Spring, and the weather had warmed up a tad. As I opened the bedroom door, hundreds of black ants crawled all over the hardwood floor. At first, I began to panic, but then I gained my senses, and I said:

"Ants, out now; this is not your house; it is my house, and I am telling you now to go back outside where you belong." I shut the bedroom door and took the dog on a long walk.

It was about 7 pm when we got home. I opened the door to the bedroom where the uninvited eusocial things were. Ants are some of the most social critters on God's earth, like wasps. That must be why they love picnics so much. Where were they? I was overjoyed and stunned as my wood floor gleamed in the evening sun. I lived in that house for another eight years and never saw those ants again. Ants must have good memories. At the very least, they knew I meant what I said, and it was the truth.

The next day, I felt the nudge to take daily communion. Again, Christ's promise to his disciples intrigued me—profound yet simple.

> And he took bread, gave thanks, and broke it, and gave unto them, saying, This is my body which is given for you: this do in remembrance of me. Likewise, also the cup after supper, saying, This cup is the new testament in my blood, which is shed for you.
>
> — LUKE 22: 19- 20

Whoever eats My flesh and drinks My blood remains in Me, and I in him.

— JOHN 6:56

I can tell you I will never stop my daily dedication to the Lord with communion. Are you entirely in command of your words, or do you often feel remorseful at what flew out of your mouth? The best you can do is apologize to the person and repent to God.

Out of your heart, your mouth speaks.

Out of the abundance of the heart the mouth speaketh.

— MATTHEW 12:34

And now, brethren, I commend you to God and the word of his grace, which can build you up and give you an inheritance among all that are sanctified.

— ACT 20:32

For by grace are ye saved through faith; and that not of yourselves: it is the gift of God: Not of works, lest any man should boast. We are his creation, created in Christ Jesus unto good works, which God ordained that we should walk in them.

— EPHESIAN 2:8-10

If you have yet to become someone who acknowledges Christ as your savior, here is a suggestion. I am almost sure you glimpsed God as a child. I say this because you may feel as far away from God as possible. And maybe you are. Seek the child within yourself, find a picture of yourself as a child, and let that be your calling card to God. Start the conversation. God never minds when His people ask questions. Particularly heartfelt questions. You can begin by thanking Him for getting you to your current age. Thank Him for your offspring, spouse, job, and future.

Offer yourself to Him. Give Him whatever you have to work with as He sees fit. Let Him know you trust Him and know He is the creator of the Universe who gave His only Begotten son who died for your sins so that you may live free. Tell Him you want your life to count for something meaningful to God. You don't need the approval of men. You want to begin to walk in His blessing alone, and He will straighten all paths on the road ahead for you.

Ask Him to teach you. Tell Him you are a willing pupil of Christ's teachings and the Holy Spirit. Then, you can ask Him to help you believe in the works Jesus did when he died on the cross for your sins. There is no shortage of God's grace; by that grace, you can know God, His son Jesus, and the Holy Spirit, for the three are one.

> Jesus said to him, 'I am the way, truth, and the life; no one comes to the Father except through Me.
>
> — JOHN 14:6

> And we all, with unveiled faces, beholding the glory of the Lord, are being transformed into the same image from one degree of glory to another. For this comes from the Lord who is the Spirit.
>
> — 2 CORINTHIANS 3;18

> For behold, the day comes, that shall burn as an oven: and all the proud, yea and all those who do wickedly, shall be stubble; and the day that comes shall burn them up, saith the LORD of Hosts. That is it shall leave them to wither and rot.

But unto You who fear my name shall the Son of righteousness arise with healing in His wings and you shall go forth and grow up as calves of the stalls.

— MALACHI CHAPTER FOUR 1-2

As a young child, I was intrigued by the night sky, and I still am. I had a small telescope to see some of the constellations more clearly. As an adult, I was heartbroken when I heard that the NASA moon landing was unreal.

In my last year of middle school, I began asking God about His stars, the Moon, and the Sun. God's spirit told me all the stars I saw were all obedient. I am the eldest child, and I understand the importance of obedience. This statement spoke to me.

God then told me the Sun and the Moon agree with each other and God.

Are they married? I asked.

That was the first time I ever heard God chuckle. The voice of God's Spirit said, Dear Child.

We know Shepherds or Magi used the stars to find their way to the Christ child in the manger.

I had learned that pagan, ungodly religions used these celestial beings as their Gods.

It was the summer going into the tenth grade that I understood that it was perversion to look at the Stars without acknowledging God for His work creating the Stars. Stars were created as a gift for those of us on earth. God was talking to the right person who would sneak out of bed, with blanket and pillow in tow, to lay in the dark backyard to catch shooting stars as they streamed across the night sky.

2

WHO IS GOD?

God is the Creator of the universe.

The Bible says with His fingers He set the stars in the sky.

He tells the numbers of the stars; He calleth them all by their names.

— PSALM 147:4

When I consider Your heavens, the work of Your fingers. The moon and the stars, which You have set in place.

— PSALM 8:3

God is Jehovah

I Am that I Am

Lift up your eyes on high And see who has created these stars,

The One who leads forth their host by number, He calls them all by name;

Because of the greatness of His might and the strength of His power,

Not one of them is missing.

— ISAIAH 40:26

God is immutable

He is that that has been He is Perfect and Unchanging

— PSALM 102:25-27

In the beginning, you laid the foundations of the earth, and the heavens are the work of your hands. They will perish, but you remain; they will all wear out like a garment. Like clothing, you will change them and they will be discarded, But you remain the same, and your years will never end.

God is Holy

You shall be holy to me, for I the LORD am holy and have separated you from the peoples, that you should be mine

— LEVITICUS 20:26

God is Just

Righteousness and justice are the foundation of your throne; steadfast love and faithfulness go before you.

— DEUTERONOMY 32:4

God is Merciful

But if from thence thou shalt seek the Lord thy God, thou shalt find Him, if thou seek Him with all thy heart and with all thy soul. When thou art in tribulation and all these things have come upon thee, even in the latter days, if thou turn to the Lord thy God and shalt be obedient unto His voice (for the Lord thy God is a merciful God), will not forsake thee, neither destroy thee nor forget the covenant of thy fathers which He swore unto them.

— DEUTERONOMY 4: 29-31

God is Love

Beloved, let us love one another: for love is of God; and everyone that loveth is born of God, and knoweth God. He that loveth not knoweth not God; for God is love. In this was manifested the love of God toward us, because that God sent his only begotten Son into the world, that we might live through him. Herein is love, not that we loved God, but that he loved us, and sent his Son to be the propitiation for our sins. Beloved, if God so loved us, we ought also to love one another. No man hath seen God at any time. If we love one another, God dwelleth in us, and his love is perfected in us. Hereby know we that we dwell in him, and he in us, because he hath given us of his Spirit. And we have seen and do testify that the Father sent the Son to be the Savior of the world. Whosoever shall confess that Jesus is the Son of God, God dwelleth in him, and he in God. And we have known and believed the love that God hath to us. God is love, and he that dwelleth in love dwelleth in God, and God in him.

— 1 JOHN 4: 7-16

God is Transcendent

For my thoughts are not your thoughts, nor are your ways my ways, declares the LORD. For as the heavens are higher than the earth, so are my ways higher than your ways and my thoughts than your thoughts.

— ISAIAH 58: 8-9

Here is one more of my experiences to help you understand what is at stake when you aren't saved.

I had not yet worked in the Psych Unit. I was quickly growing in my faith and all the experiences I had, while I believe experiences are the best teacher, all the undesirable lessons were brought by the enemy.

I understood that God gave me a soul to be able to smell. He gave you one also.

I was with a friend and we were going to a Bible study. She pulled into a stop-and-go gas station. I waited in the car. When she hadn't come out of the store after a few minutes I got out of the car and went into the gas station.

The clerk was six feet away from the cash register behind the cigarette display and my friend was looking wild-eyed at me. He won't give me change, she said.

Then the man was suddenly in the back room completely removed from view yelling, "Just put the money on the counter." I had changed and paid the correct amount in tens, fives and one's.

We left the store.

"What is the matter with that guy?", she asked. "He has a problem and you and I alarmed him."

I do remember before being saved that I would have times when a situation was concerning and sometimes alarming. I later learned that was my soul, my sense of smell, sniffing out danger. We all have that ability.

Now with my armor on, Christ on the inside, I have no fear and great discernment. Can your mind think properly when fear runs rampant? No, because panic can set in. Panic and fear are the favorite picks of Satan's tool kit.

Once I was saved I found 1 Peter 4-9 written in 60 AD says it best (born anew) into an imperishable inheritance (beyond the reach of change) and undefiled and unfading, reserved in heaven for you who are being protected and shielded by the power of God through your faith for a salvation that is ready to be revealed (to you)in the last time. In this, you may rejoice greatly, even though now for a little while, if necessary, you have been distressed by various trials so that the greatness of your faith, which is much more precious than perishable gold, even though tested and purified by fire, may be found to result in (your) praise and glory and honor at the revelation of Christ Jesus. Though you have not seen Him you love Him; and though you do not even see you now, you believe and trust in Him and you greatly rejoice and delight with inexpressible and glorious joy receiving as the result (the outcome, the consummation) of your faith, the salvation of your souls.

God is the Great I Am, God is the deliverer of His people, God is righteous and God is wonderful.

There is nothing made on Earth that God did not make. See the Scripture in the following passages:

Exodus 3, Psalms 18, Psalm 145:17, Psalm 19:7, and *Colossians 116*

Scientists who work with DNA and its coding, more specifically, are glimpsing an understanding of the power of God's spoken word with logos in a creative endeavor. Logos is the term first systematized by Aristotle, used in Western philosophy to appeal to the act of reason that relies on logic or cause for a desired outcome.

You can find God by setting your heart, mind, and soul to it.

I praised the Holy, omniscient God. I worshipped the Only God, the Creator of the World. I thanked God for my life and all His creation. I glorified His artistry and thanked Him for His Only-begotten Son, who died for my sins.

My house shook with thunder on that bright Autumn day. The Spirit of God of the universe spoke to me and showed me many things.

The spirit voice told me about the importance of his commandments. He told me about the power of unwavering faith and said Hold On. The fact that God gave Moses the Ten Commandments did not escape my awareness as it began resonating in my soul.

I did my best to hold on. I fell into sin, and God helped me pull myself out. I thanked Him, repented, and promised I would give it my all and never be willfully disobedient again. I will never again let my obedience waiver.

God continues to speak in dreams. He has given me big things to do. I have been where I don't feel qualified, all to bring God's word. My work life remains a thing of divine endeavor.

He is God, and He will do what He sees best. He is the absolute authority, and His word is His truth. To have genuine faith in God, you must understand He is Holy. He is excellent, trustworthy, and filled with Grace.

His love for you is beyond measure. You don't deserve His Love, and neither do I. We must live Holy, obedient lives. We must ask God what, Dear Father, I must do today that only I can do for Your Majesty. Then, we must listen and act.

We must offer love, knowing that we are not to judge others as we stand at the line of what God wants. We are to please God and God alone, not man or man's ideas.

Emotions should not run your life or make your decisions. Unforgiveness, hate, and anger are all emotions. Ask God to help you manage your feelings, and thank Him for helping you.

I realize we don't know what we are missing. Thankfully, God took me from one American coast to another to find churches that welcome the Spirit of God into their services. Once you sit in the presence of the Holy Spirit, you will find greater truth and Freedom. Yours will be Freedom from worry, anxiety, or concern. All things look possible. Once you have an experience like this, nothing else will satisfy you. I can't explain it, just like I can't tell you how delicious grilled fruit on vanilla ice cream is.

3

HE KNOWS YOU

The best process I know to raise your self-esteem and view of yourself is when you decide to believe that it is God's image in whom you are created.

So God created Man in His image. In the image of God, He created

them, male and female.

God created angels to do the will of God, to worship God, and to help those of us on earth.

The Man was created a little higher than the angels.

— GENESIS 1:27

And of the Angels He said, Who makes His Angles Spirits and His ministers a flame of fire.

— HEBREWS 1:7

Hebrews is a lovely Bible book, which contains thirteen Chapters that some believe were written by Paul in AD 64. It is sometimes referred to as the Faith book. Hebrews discusses the New Covenant as unsimilar to the Mosaic Covenant that Moses used when the captivities were set free from Egypt.

But now has He obtained a more excellent ministry (This new covenant is based on the blood of Christ and replaces the old covenant in animal blood) by how much also He is the mediator of a Better Covenant, which was established on Better Promises. (The New Covenant is explicitly based on the cleansing and forgiveness of all sin, which the Old Covenant could not do.)

For that First Covenant had been faultless, then should no place have been sought for the second.

For finding fault with them, He said Behold, these days come, saith the Lord, when I will make a New Covenant with the House of Israel and with the House of Judah.

Not according to the covenant they made with their fathers, in the days when I took them by the hand to lead them out of the land of Egypt; because they continued not in My Covenant, and I regarded them not, says the Lord.

For this is the New Covenant that I will make with the House of Israel after those days, saith the Lord; I will put My Laws into their mind and write them in their hearts, and I will be to them a God, and they shall be to me, MY people.

— HEBREW 8:6-10

The New Covenant is:

A new Priest- Jesus

A New Covenant

A Better Promise

Long ago, at many times and in many ways, God spoke to our fathers by the prophets, but in these last days he has spoken to us by his Son, whom he appointed the heir of all things, through whom also he created the worlds Who being the brightness of His Glory, and the express image of His Person and upholding All things by the Word of His Power., for when He had by himself purged our sins, sat down on the Right Hand of the Majesty on high.

— HEBREWS 1:1-3

He is the radiance of the glory of God and the exact imprint of his nature, and he upholds the universe by the word of his power. Christ was crucified, died, and buried and on the third day, He was raised from the dead. His whipped body took thirty-nine lashes for our sickness, and going to Hell He conquered death and the grave. He rose to Heaven where He sat down at the right hand of God the Father.

For whosoever (anyone anywhere) shall call upon the Name of the Lord shall be saved.

— PAUL SAYS IN THE BOOK OF ROMANS 10: 13

So then Faith comes by hearing and hearing By the Word of God.

— ROMANS 10:17

But as He which has called you as Holy, so be ye Holy in all manner of conversation

Because it is written, Be ye Holy, for I Am Holy.

— PETER 1:15-16

I have refrained my feet from every evil way, that I might keep your word.

— PSALMS 119:101

When you become a new man, a new woman in Christ, you will still be the same person, but the sinful nature that lived within you, placed there when Adam fell in the garden, is now absent. When you give your life to Christ, you will be sanctified. To be washed by the blood of Christ (a metaphor) with newness comes from praying repentance and salvation in faith, which ushers in the washing of your soul.

You won't believe nor be able to remember who you were when you lived in a sinful state. A deliverance prayer by another is needed if you have willfully partnered with the forces of darkness. Routine Drug use would be one such case. Unfortunately, I cannot provide a deliverance prayer you can use on yourself as your will allowed the demons a place of residence.

If you are chanting, which provides effects, you must decide to turn away from the darkness. You can find a deliverance minister to pray over the phone with you. I would not wait for the enemy to seek, kill, and destroy you.

I was reading the bible as I prayed one day, and the Spirit's voice asked what I thought about verse 3:16. Of course, John 3:16 was the first verse that popped into my head was John 3:16.

For God so loved the world that He gave His Only Begotten Son, that whosoever believes in Him will not die but have Everlasting Life.

God impressed upon me to go from chapter to chapter in the New Testament and note Chapter 3: 16 verses. I was familiar with John 3:16, and with a historical look, it could be interesting to see how the first disciples carried on after the Lord's crucifixion and death. They called their belief group the Way and never claimed to be a religion but a band of believers.

Here are all the 3:16 verses in the New Testament. Malachi being the last book of the Old Testament is where I started looking at verses 3:16.

I perused the Bible noting all the 3:16 scriptures aside from Hebrews 3:16, which says there will be those who don't believe the others, which seems to reference a cliff note style of the broader view and understanding of the work of Jesus.

> Then those who feared the Lord spoke to one another, and the Lord gave attention and heard it, and a book of remembrance was written before Him for those who fear the Lord and who esteem His name.
>
> — MALACHI 3:16

I see us as the body of Christ renewing that stance. The time in which we live calls for the unification of all believers without hindrance walking in love and grace to do the works of God in these end-time days.

> And Jesus, when he was baptized, went up straightway out of the water: and, lo, the heavens were opened unto him, and he saw the Spirit of God descending like a dove, and lighting upon him.
>
> — MATTHEW 3:16

These are the twelve he appointed: Simon (to whom he gave the name Peter).

— MARK 3:16

John the Baptist answered them all, saying, "I baptize you with water, but he who is mightier than I is coming, the strap of whose sandals I am not worthy to untie. He will baptize you with the Holy Spirit and fire."

— LUKE 3:16

ESV: And his name—by faith in his name—has made this man strong whom you see and know, and the faith through Jesus has given the Man this perfect health in your presence.

— ACTS 3:16

Destruction and misery *are* in their ways

— ROMANS 3:16

Don't you know that you are God's temple, and God's Spirit dwells in your midst?

The church is a unique body because it is set apart by God to be a display of His character.

— 1 CORINTHIANS 3:16

Paul continues to make the case that faith in Christ is all that is required to be justified—"made righteous"—in God's eyes.

— GALATIANS 3:16

Proclaims the fact that all people, Jew and Gentile, can now be part of the same spiritual family

— EPHESIANS 3:16

Nevertheless, whereto we have already attained, let us walk by the same rule; let us mind the same thing.

— PHILIPPIANS 3:16

Let the word of Christ dwell in you richly, teaching and admonishing one another in all wisdom, singing psalms and hymns and spiritual songs, with thankfulness in your hearts to God.

— COLOSSIANS 3:16

The peace I give to you. Not the peace the world gives do I give to you. Do not let your heart be troubled, neither let it be afraid.

Now may the Lord of peace Himself continually grant you peace in every circumstance. The Lord be with you all!

— 1-2 THESSALONIANS 3:16

And without controversy, great is the mystery of godliness: God was manifest in the flesh, justified in the Spirit, seen of angels, preached unto the Gentiles, believed on in the world, received up into glory.

All Scripture is inspired by God and profitable for teaching, reproof, correction, and righteousness training.

— 1-2 TIMOTHY 3:16

For some, when they heard, did provoke

—HEBREWS 3:16

For where envying and strife are, there is confusion, and every evil work

—JAMES 3:16

Having a good conscience; that, whereas they speak evil of you, as of evildoers, they may be ashamed they falsely accuse your good conversation in Christ.

He writes the same Way in all his letters, speaking in them of these matters. His letters contain some things that are hard to understand, which ignorant and unstable people distort, as they do the other Scriptures, to their destruction.

—1-2 PETER 3:16

For God so loved the world, that he gave His only begotten Son, that whosoever believeth in him should not perish, but have everlasting life.

—JOHN 3:16

So, because you are lukewarm - neither hot nor cold - I am about to spit you out of my mouth.

—REV 3:16

I mentioned that as a nurse, I never minded working where the line between life and death was clinically evident. I was always in prayer or pleading with God for his intervention. I always felt a strong presence of God in that place. I also mentioned that God took me to different places to hear testimonies of people often as they encountered God. One had perhaps one foot in Hell. (God explained this to me as a bull's eye on their back.) Therefore, these three men's testimonies are suitable for this discussion. These test subjects are men. Women do not hold the upper hand. Going to Hell is an equal-opportunity endeavor.

As the nurse in the code near the line of life and death, I never felt the shiver of Hell. It never occurred to me that all of these folks had some connection to God. The following people I would encounter were not as connected to God as they needed to be when death came calling. If a person is on death's door from drug use, this is what I heard.

He knew he was addicted to drugs. He had a rough childhood, and the internal pain was indescribable. The drugs took that pain away. This patient heard God say stop. He knew it was God. And he said to the Lord he'd like to finish his purchase. Moments later, the Lord became angry and displayed anger. The man said God maltreated him, or so he thought. What might be going on here?

I instantly decided that Satan might be hovering when death comes. Of course, the Lord will always show up, but I do not believe you will see anger from Christ other than the story in scripture about the money changers in the Temple. Christ, after all, died for us, wishing that none would perish.

> Then Jesus went into the temple of God, drove out all those who bought and sold in the temple, and overturned the tables of the money changers and the seats of those who sold doves.
>
> — MATT 13 : 21: 12-13

My psych patients heard regularly from Satan. The voice of the Spirit told me he has special mercy for people with mental and other neurological issues, preventing the straightforward and logical ability to have strong faith. For that, I am immensely thankful. I counseled those who had attempted to take their own life to repent to God for following the leadings of Satan to kill themselves.

Pride goes before destruction and a haughty spirit before a fall.

— MATTHEW 21; 12-13 PROVERBS 15:18

So your prayer would be

> *Dear Lord,*
> *Thank you that I was created in my mother's womb*
> *to be the man I am, though sinning. Lord, rip*
> *out the roots of Pride from my life. Give me a*
> *new heart to continue my conquests without fear*
> *and with renewed strength. I repent for my sins*
> *and have lived so much of my life without you.*
> *Save me now as I confess my gratitude that Your*
> *Son, Christ died on the cross for my sin. I ask in*
> *Jesus's name. Create in me a new man*
> *today. Amen*

After hearing this, I understood that you are relaxed and in control without a care in the world or commitment to God until the moment of death hits you. Then all bets are off. I think this is the one foot in Hell example. Thankfully, he lived to talk about it.

The following person was turning his back on God over a specific situation. He did not pray about his actions. He just did what his heart told him. Myopic sight, perhaps. Oh Boy! He found himself at death's door. He heard God and Satan speak. He did not realize it was Satan until some time had passed. Satan said Just let go. He did not do as Satan suggested. He did describe that when one is in the throes of death, it is a solo journey. You have no cognition of your earthy connections or your mortgage amount. What he did see was a scene Jesus wanted him to see. Earthlings are not allowed to poke around Heaven without being accompanied. I heard that several times. If you are even allowed into Heaven, it is to show you one thing.

What he saw were two widely spread mountain plateaus. He was on one side with an Angel beside him, and "they" were on the other. They represented a steady stream of people walking as if going to a concert venue. They were all over eighteen, so it seemed; some of them were grannies. They were all mouthing off with anger and a begrudging demeanor as they shuffled along and walked right off the edge to what he knew was the pit.

Hold no anger or malice in your heart. Ask for God to remove the bitterness. Turn to God for love. Don't put the present nor your eternal future at risk because of an emotion.

Believe me; I understand that emotion is created to keep us safe (fear) and give us joy and should not be allowed to go rogue, unchecked, and put you in a stewing fit over who knows what? I see that as a cheap shot from Satan.

The third man lost control of his life in a boating event as he worked to fix the underneath of a bridge as a part of his job. From what I saw, he was a burly man who could successfully wrestle a bear.

I feel for your type, competent at everything. You may think you don't need God. You could not be more incorrect. If you are living without Christ, Satan knows it, and like a tiger, he lays in wait, or worse yet, he sets you up.

My job required me to go immediately to a hospital to check on a critically injured person. Unfortunately, I rarely had good information, as I drove a reasonable distance to the Hospital. A misspelled last name, no date of birth, and an employer name. No claim number, and no documents other than my business card. Hospitals have HIPPA down pat, and I respect that; however, HIPPA has no legal means under worker comp to deny information at times of injury. The lack of qualifying data means I must be sweet and soft to get some info.

I was immediately rebuffed by the health establishment this fall day. I returned to my car to pray. This man had a family with him. Despite the situation, I prayed for everyone that the Grace of God would overwhelm them. I prayed I would also have the Grace to bring light into the dark as needed. I did sense a dark presence. I sat quietly in my car as I waited for God. Then it came like a movie clip flashing before my eyes. And I knew more about this man in ten seconds than I cared to. He had discarded God long ago. I prayed God would have mercy on his soul and that he would obtain a shot at Heaven, and I meant it.

Suppose you have discarded God if you do not thank God occasionally. Suppose you have left jagged rocks for others to contend with while you seek a better life. I can tell you that it is a dangerous place to be. I would have never known that Satan rested at the edge of life, waiting to snatch your soul if you were outright sinning or, at the very least, giving GOD no thanks, no honor, and zero prayers. The Bible says we in Heaven will not know those we love who are not with us, for there is no sorrow in Heaven.

You can go daily and skip along the path of life with joy and wanderlust until Satan and his minions realize your easy game. If that is the case, you may know and obey one commandment. Do you have a bullseye on your back?

Will you know what to do if you get your lights knocked out in the most severe sense imaginable? Will you even have time, or will Satan crowd into that space between life and death and scramble your mind so you can't think straight as he carts your soul to his pit?

Do you have any idea about the call on your life? I'm too old; I'm beyond help. That is a lie if I ever heard one. The Bible is filled with stories of people God used for great things. Your second prayer after you give your life to Christ can be to show you how you can be used by God. God can speak to you through prophetic words, dreams, and what we will call hunches.

Today's time is scary because everyone with Spiritual understanding knows the clock is counting down. God never intended that Hell would welcome humans. The only permanent residents were to be Satan and his minions.

Sadly, many humans aren't allowed in Heaven when the end of life comes. God wishes that none would perish. Heaven does not permit corrupted things beyond its gates. Unrepented sinful nature is not allowed in Heaven.

Preaching Fire and Brim Stone has its place in the world today because the hour is getting late. However, I would be remiss not to inform you that your remaining days on earth can be grand and joy-filled when you repent for wasting your life on sin. Only God can erase your darkest days so that the peace that passes all understanding will be yours today.

In the Bible, David was a warrior and a worshiper of God. They say he could jump straight on and scale a 7-foot wall. While fighting the Philistines, David jumped up with his sword, got the enemy at the jugular, pulled his sword out, and took out the next giant.

They had an excavation near Calgary Hill in Israel and found a sword of a Philistine.

The sword was 5 feet 2 inches long—I know exactly how long it was—but that did not deter David.

For all his brawn, David was a lover of God; he knew his success depended on a dependency on God.

You can be burly and capable and even drive a Harley, and knowing that Pride rivals Heaven is essential.

So this man landed in the vestibule of Hell after He took his last breath of earthly air. (he didn't know it, but I suspected it based on another patient's testimony.) I had only heard one other person mention such a thing. It was dark, he could hear horrible noises, and the stench of rot and smoke was the worst.

He could see the light in the distance, and people were walking by on the other side. He said it was solitary, and he had a passing thought that his mother and his wife were praying for him. He lay on a gurney in the ED after being coded with an oxygen mask on. His wife and mother were in the hall, anxious to see him. Then, realizing their prayers had been answered, they rushed to him as he lay there.

He realized his mother's prayers held the most power. He has no plans for future water sports. I sensed he was still grappling with the ordeal and what it meant. Thankfully, there was a small degree of physical damage to his mortal body.

Not one of us knows what tomorrow holds. Don't fall asleep one more night without talking to God. Consider journaling. I journal daily, and I tell you honestly that my guardian angel must read English. This I know.

God needs thanksgiving, praise, obedience, and an honest attempt at holiness and worship.

4

MANY ROADS, ONLY ONE WAY

Pentecostal emphasis is a direct personal experience with God through the Baptism of the Holy Spirit. Lutheran, Episcopalian, Catholic, Protestant, and Methodist all believe in Christ Crucified and they represent a sect of religion. The term Pentecostal is derived from the biblical event of Pentecost when the believers of the Way, as they denied a religion and followed Jesus's instruction to wait in the upper room for the Promise of the Father.

> And behold, I send the Promise of My Father upon you, but tarry not ye in the city of Jerusalem, until you are endued with power from on high.
>
> — LUKE 49:29

One hundred and twenty believers were in attendance. There are fifty days between Passover and Pentecost. Some have taken Jesus's time in the tomb with his forty days of Ascension, believing the group waited ten days in the upper room. This group did not describe themselves as a religion. They were simply a group of believers who loved God and Christ.

It is important to note that as it relates to Acts 1:13, The wealthy of Jerusalem resided in the Upper City, so rooms were more spacious. Ancient texts report gatherings of large numbers of sages in more spacious upper rooms.

You may decide to obtain a bible background reference bible. That, along with an Expositors Study Bible in the King James Version, will give you a broader understanding of the scriptures. The accounts, seen through the Jewish cultural lens, lend a greater sense of the biblical text. Understanding how Jesus selected the disciples of varied cultures is quite fascinating.

Add that to the many Gods Judaism had and place it alongside the Pagan religion of the Romans. So the disciples found themselves in Roman Courts trying to state their case and avoid landmines of other firmly held beliefs as they knew the truth through the living Christ.

I can't help but think about when the eldest siblings knew Santa did not exist while the younger kids still believed. How hard was it for the most senior siblings not to spill the beans? Based on the child's personality, it was nearly impossible.

When you know the truth, its power can blow out of your mouth at will. It may even cost you a job. It happened one summer day. I felt like I had won the lottery after being released to go free for speaking the truth. I didn't roll into a meadow of daisies, but I was free. I thanked God for it.

The disciples were often dragged to court and questioned by the rulers of the time. Each one, except for John, was martyred because of his words of truth. We cannot let fear lead our actions or beliefs. God promises great things to those who believe and are obedient. The joy and miraculous events, big and small, can fill you with awe and wanderlust and steal your heart in the most tender of ways.

No, you don't deserve the love Christ gives expressly to you, and neither do I. The cross makes this an issue that does not need discussion or lengthy debate. It is more tender than that. God's only Son was sent expressly to this world so *you* would know the love of the Father and the hope of his calling for your life and your life alone. Pardon me, but what are you waiting for?

Consider Act 1 1-26, Written in the message bible.

Dear Theophilus, in the first volume of this book, I wrote about everything that Jesus began to do and teach until the day he said goodbye to the apostles, the ones he had chosen through the Holy Spirit and was taken up to heaven. After his death, he presented himself alive to them in many different settings over forty days. In face-to-face meetings, he talked to them about things concerning the kingdom of God. As they met and ate meals together, he told them that they were on no account to leave Jerusalem but "must wait for what the Father promised: the promise you heard from me. John baptized in water; you will be baptized in the Holy Spirit. And soon." When they were together for the last time, they asked, "Master, are you going to restore the kingdom to Israel now? Is this the time?" He told them, "You don't get to know the time. Timing is the Father's business. What you'll get is the Holy Spirit. And when the Holy Spirit comes on you, you will be able to be my witnesses in Jerusalem, all over Judea and Samaria, even to the ends of the world." These were his last words. As they watched, he was taken up and disappeared in a cloud. They stood there, staring into the empty sky. Suddenly two men appeared—in white robes! They said, "You Galileans!—why do you just stand here looking up at an empty sky? This very Jesus who was taken up from among you to heaven will come as certainly—and mysteriously—as he left."

So they left the mountain called Olives and returned to Jerusalem. It was a little over half a mile. They went to the upper room they had been using as a meeting place: These are the twelve disciples of Christ.

— ACTS 1:1-26

Review the list and make notations about how they were called to Christ and how they displayed their faith rather than through actions or words or both. Do a Google search and find many scriptural references and attributes.

Peter-

____

John-

____

James-

____

Andrew-

____

Philip-

____

Thomas-

____

Bartholomew-

Matthew-

James, Son of Alphaeus:

Simon the Zealot:

Judas, Son of James-Thaddeus:

They agreed they were in this for good, completely together in prayer, the women included. Also, Jesus' mother, Mary, and his brothers. During this time, Peter stood up in the company—about 120 of them in the room at the time—and said, "Friends, long ago the Holy Spirit spoke through David regarding Judas, who became the guide to those who arrested Jesus. That Scripture had to be fulfilled, and now has been. Judas was one of us and had his assigned place in this ministry. "He took the evil bribe money and bought a small farm. There he came to a bad end, rupturing his belly and spilling his guts. Everybody in Jerusalem knows this by now; they call the place Murder Meadow. It's exactly what we find written in the Psalms:

Let his farm become haunted
So no one can ever live there.
"And also what was written later:
Let someone else take over his post.

"Judas must now be replaced. The replacement must come from the company of men who stayed together with us from the time Jesus was baptized by John up to the day of his Ascension, designated along with us as a witness to his resurrection." They nominated two: Joseph Barsabbas nicknamed Justus, and Matthias. Then they prayed, "You, O God, know every one of us inside and out. Make plain which of these two men you choose to take place in this ministry and leadership that Judas threw away to go his Way." They then drew straws. Matthias won and was counted in with the eleven apostles.

When the day of Pentecost came, they were all together in one place. Suddenly a sound like the blowing of a violent wind came from heaven and filled the whole house where they were sitting.

They saw what seemed to be tongues of fire that separated and came to rest on each of them. All of them were filled with the Holy Spirit and began to speak in other tongues, as the Spirit enabled them.

— ACTS 2:1-4

And these signs shall follow them that believe; In my name shall they cast out devils; they shall speak with new tongues; they shall take up serpents; and if they drink any deadly thing, it shall not hurt them; they shall lay hands on the sick, and they shall recover.

— MARK 16:17-18

The day is soon coming if it is not already here. The day when millions cry out to know Christ. I feel it in my bones. Will we as adults in Christ not judge? Like a cafeteria lady who has Jesus by her side. That is the kind of "adults" who will help the youth who are set on fire by their King. Those who need to know more of Him, not a religion but Christ crucified.

But of those things, which God before had showed by the mouth of all His Prophets, that Christ should suffer, He has so fulfilled Repent ye therefore, and be converted, that your sins may be blotted out when the times for refreshing shall come from the presence of the Lord.

And He shall send Jesus Christ, which before was preached to you, Whom the Heavens must receive until the times of restitution of all things, which God has spoken by the mouth of all His Holy Prophets since the world began.

— ACTS 3: 18-21

Enter ye in at the strait gate: for wide is the gate, and broad is the Way, that leadeth to destruction, and many there be which go in there after. Because strait is the gate, and narrow is the Way, which leadeth unto life, and few there be that find it. Beware of false prophets, which come to you in sheep's clothing, but inwardly they are ravening wolves. Ye shall know them by their fruits. Do men gather grapes of thorns; or figs of thistles? Even so, every good tree bringeth forth good fruit, but a corrupt tree bringeth forth evil fruit. A good tree cannot bring forth evil fruit, neither can a corrupt tree bring forth good fruit. Every tree that bringeth not forth good fruit is hewn down, and cast into the fire. Wherefore by their fruits, ye shall know them.

— MATT 7:13-20

Anyone of us has access to God only through Christ Jesus. Our access to Christ is by way of the Cross. Christ, crucified in the most heinous sense, accomplished the Father's task of taking care of Satan for His children's sake while giving His Son all authority on Heaven and Earth. Believing in HIM Jesus and acknowledging His Death and Resurrection, having conquered Hell, raised from the dead to sit at the Father's Right Hand. It is the person of Jesus we follow and adore while denying ourselves. We do not live our own lives but with Christ in us. John says it best in his Gospel in the first book of John.

> In the beginning was the Word, and the Word was with God, and the Word was God. The same was true at the beginning with God. All things were made by him, and without him was not anything made that was made. In him was life; and the life was the light of men. And the light shineth in darkness; and the darkness comprehended it not. There was a man sent from God, whose name was John. The same came for a witness, to bear witness of the Light, that all men through him might believe. He was not that Light, but was sent to bear witness of that Light. That was the true Light, which lightest every man that cometh into the world. He was in the world, and the world was made by him, and the world knew him not. He came unto his own, and his own received him not. But as many as received him, to them gave the power to become the sons of God, even to them that believe on his name: Which were born, not of blood, nor of the will of the flesh, nor the will of man, but of God. And the Word was made flesh and dwelt among us, (and we beheld his glory, the glory as of the only begotten of the Father) full of grace and truth.

> — JOHN 1: 1-14

> Saying, The Son of man must suffer many things, be rejected by the elders and chief priests and scribes, be slain, and be raised on

the third day. And he said to them, " If any man will come after me, let him deny himself, take up his cross daily, and follow me. For whosoever will save his life shall lose it: but whosoever will lose his life for my sake, the same shall save it.

— LUKE 9:22

The way is alive with light, truth, and grace. Anything accustomed to being done in daylight is notable. Compared to when the cover of darkness accomplishes a task, the action immediately draws suspicion. I think of the shipment of people as a terrible thought as we pray to end child trafficking. Think of how many things have happened in this current day in darkness. Every country that ever abolished its government's currency did so in the dark. The people would retire for the day only to wake in the morning to find that their money system had failed. As long as ungodly humans run governments, I suppose no government is immune from pulling this deceptive act.

Let's talk for a minute about the need for a bible to use as you read, learn, and grow in your understanding of God. The only way to know God is to read His word, which is life. The Old Testament I and II Chronicles show David, a worshiper of God and a man with a heart for God. David is a man, and he fell to sin. Chronicles talks about David the King, who works with God with reverence; his sin remains because Jesus has not yet died on the cross. It is a good story about God's character and that of David.

I use a King James Expositor Study Bible for most of my reading and confer with the Amplified Bible, where I enjoy a more extraordinary text with many translations included when needed, or the NIV (New International) translation. The Message Bible may be easy to read, but it does not give me the details I seek. Yet, with its contemporary language style, it provides an easy under-standing of some Bible stories.

I suspect you will dream more once you get to know God as I did. I bought several dream interpretation books; the best is "Understanding the Dreams You Dream" by Ira Milligan. If English is not your first language, Wycliff is a Bible translation company with the Holy Bible translated into hundreds of languages. Visit Wycliffe.Org for more information.

5

GOD'S CREATION

Listen as you read the words of Ezekiel, the prophet. Ezekiel is to give a word to the prince of Tyrus. There is a reference to the Garden of Eden in this chapter. Whom do you think God is referencing here? There is some pretty strong language coming for God. This is the God who is a consuming fire and calls for fear of the Lord. He will be recognized as Almighty God.

Again, the Word of the Lord came unto me, saying Son of man, take up a dirge (funeral poem to be sung) for the king of Tyrus, and say to him, Thus Says the Lord God, You had the full measure of perfection and the finishing touches (of completeness) Full of wisdom and perfect in beauty. You were in Eden the Garden of God: Every precious stone was your covering, The ruby, the topaz, and the diamond. The beryl, the onyx, and the jasper: the lapis lazuli, the turquoise, and the emerald. And the gold; the workmanship of your settings and your sockets, was in you. They were prepared for you on the day you were created. You were the anointed Cherub who covers and protects. And I have placed you there. You were on the Holy mountain of God, You walked amid the stones of the fire. You were blameless in your ways from the day that you were created. Until unrighteousness and evil were found in you. Through the abundance of your commerce, you were internally filled with lawlessness and violence. And you have sinned. Therefore I cast you out as profane and unholy thing From the mountain of God; And I have destroyed you O covering Cherub, from the midst of the stones of the fire. Your heart was proud and arrogant because of your beauty; You destroyed your wisdom for the sake of your splendor: I cast you to the ground, I lay you before kings, That they may look you. You have profaned your sanctuaries By the great quantities of your sins, and the enormity of your guilt, By the unrighteousness of your trade. Therefore will have brought forth a fire from your midst; It has consumed you, And I have reduced you to ashes upon the Earth in the sight of all who look at you. All the people (nations) who knew you Are appalled at you; you have come to a horrible and terrifying end And will forever cease to be.

— EZEKIEL CHAPTER 28; 11-20 HOLY
AMPLIFIED BIBLE

O give thanks unto the Lord; for he is good: because his mercy endures forever.

Let Israel now say, that his mercy endures forever.

Let the house of Aaron now say, that his mercy endures forever.

Let them now that fear the Lord say, that his mercy endures forever.

I called upon the Lord in distress: the Lord answered me- and set me in a large place.

The Lord is on my side; I will not fear: what can man do unto me?

The Lord taketh my part with them that help me: therefore shall I see my desire upon them that hate me.

It is better to trust in the Lord than to put confidence in man.

It is better to trust in the Lord than to put confidence in princes.

All nations compassed me about: but in the name of the Lord will I destroy them.

They compassed me about; yea, they compassed me about but in the name of the Lord I will destroy them.

They compassed me about like bees: they are quenched as the fire of thorns: for in the name of the Lord, I will destroy them.

Thou hast thrust sore at me that I might fall: but the Lord helped me.

The Lord is my strength and song; and has become my salvation.

The voice of rejoicing and salvation is in the tabernacles of the righteous: the right hand of the Lord doeth valiantly.

The right hand of the Lord is exalted: the right hand of the Lord doeth valiantly.

I shall not die, but live, and declare the works of the Lord.

The Lord hath chastened me sore: but he hath not given me over unto death.

Open to me the gates of righteousness: I will go into them, and I will praise the Lord:

This gate of the Lord, into which the righteous shall enter.

I will praise thee: for thou hast heard me, and art become my salvation.

The stone which the builders refused; becomes the headstone of the corner.

This is the Lord's doing; it is marvelous in our eyes.

This is the day which the Lord hath made; we will rejoice and be glad in it.

Save now, I beseech thee, O Lord: O Lord, I beseech thee, send now prosperity.

Blessed be he that cometh in the name of the Lord: we have blessed you out of the house of the Lord.

God is the Lord, which hath showed us light: bind the sacrifice with cords, even unto the horns of the altar.

Thou art my God, and I will praise thee: thou art my God, I will exalt thee.

O give thanks unto the Lord; for he is good: for his mercy endures forever.

— PSALMS 118; 1-29

Thy word is a lamp unto my feet: and a light unto my path.

— PSALMS 119-105

I will remember the deeds of the LORD; yes, I will remember your miracles of long ago. I will consider all your works and meditate on all your mighty deeds.

— PSALMS 77:11-12, NEW INTERNATIONAL
VERSION (NIV)

And I appeared unto Abraham, unto Isaac, and Jacob, by the name of God Almighty, but by my name, Jehovah was I not known to them.

These are names used for GOD throughout the New Testament in the Hebrew texts as **Elohim and Jehovah.**

Jesus named Lord in the Old Testament mentioned 600 times as **Yahweh or Adonai.**

— EXODUS 6:3

When Jesus came to the region of Caesarea Philippi, he asked his disciples, "Who do people say the Son of Man is?" They replied, "Some say John the Baptist; others say Elijah; and still others, Jeremiah or one of the prophets."

"But what about you?" he asked. "Who do you say I am?"

Simon Peter answered, "You are the Messiah, the Son of the living God."

— MATTHEW 16: 13-16

Jesus and his disciples went on to the villages around Caesarea Philippi. On the Way he asked them, "Who do people say I am?"

They replied, "Some say John the Baptist; others say Elijah; and still others, one of the prophets."

"But what about you?" he asked. "Who do you say I am?"

Peter answered, "You are the Messiah."

— MARK 8:27-29

Once when Jesus was praying in private and his disciples were with him, he asked them, "Who do the crowds say I am?"

They replied, "Some say John the Baptist; others say Elijah; and still others, that one of the prophets of long ago has come back to life."

"But what about you?" he asked. "Who do you say I am?"

Peter answered, "God's Messiah."

— LUKE 9: 18-20

Why was Jesus asking about who the people thought He was? He didn't ask what the ruling class, The Pharisees, and the Roman rulers thought. He already knew that. He came to save the people. He wanted the people to know the truth as they were being fed lies like we were being fed lies. So many people missed Jesus even though word had spread far and wide about Him during the three years of His ministry.

Seventy years after Jesus' death, Israel was invaded, and the second Temple that Cyrus decreed and Herod had started and his Son Solomon completed lay in ruins. Do you think Jesus could see that far into the future? Of course, he could because GOD knows the end from the beginning.

I make known the end from the beginning,

from ancient times, what is still to come.

I say, 'My purpose will stand,

and I will do all that I please.'

— ISAIAH 46:10

If we knew the painstaking effort to ensure the Bible contained only the words inspired by the Godhead, written by the disciples of Jesus who preached the word to bring repentance and new birth, we would be amazed.

The solemn task of the Biblical scribes was the accurate chronicling of the words spoken by the Holy Spirit by the disciples. I picture those men in traditional dress sitting at long tables with paper scrolls all around. Tasks of fact-checking previously written works provided the necessary corroboration so that the scribbling process could continue. Biblical scholars mention that Paul and other disciples leave clues in their writings that outsiders came in to take the penned words of Paul's speech, and these outsiders were often men of the legal class. These men relied on the truth, and no doubt had a strong sense of the necessity to keep the factual truth for the scribes to work with. In this case, they played the role of messenger, delivering the words spoken by Paul to be submitted. Then, using a hot wax stamp, most likely in the lawyer's presence, Paul the Apostle indicates the original spoken words. No wonder these men assisted in getting the gospels into the Holy Bible.

The Book of Titus 3rd chapter verses 1-3 gives one example. Bring Zenas, the lawyer, and Apollos diligently on their journey so that nothing will be lacking for them.

These were dangerous times with many false actors in the lands. Actors desiring to deceive the public and put shame on Christ's story. They were attempting by false pretenses to lead people from believing the works that Jesus did.

As we continue to imagine, as I indicated in the first book of the series, when I became aware of God's love for me and my desire to follow him completely, I will walk in righteousness, not perfect but repentant, ever mindful of what Christ did for me.

I was hungry for the things of God. I mentioned I went to a Christian bookstore in Florida and bought ten books, hoping to find the way to God in the pages. I did not find what I sought, so I sought TV Evangelists.

Today, you have YouTube. I write this as a warning, a severe concern for you as you perhaps seek the truth of the gospel for the first time. Tiff Shuttlesworth has an excellent YouTube Bible Study.

The claim is the ministry of many preachers, who said if you want God to act in your life, pay up. These ministries are across America, from Texas to Chicago and Florida. I was getting biblical teaching in most cases; however, a heavy dose of you can buy this promise from God donate here.

Not long after, I obtained the job God opened for me in the Psych Unit. I worked hard and earned good vacation time. Then, God dragged me around to get the teaching He wanted me to hear. It was Pentecostal teaching He sent me to, and I sucked it up like a dry sponge.

The other day on YouTube, I heard a man holding a red Bible saying there were two kinds of tongues. He quoted the Gifts of the Spirit Discernment of Tongues passage. 1 Corinthians 12:1 8-11. He then volunteered he had been in a demonic cult, and he was now on fire for God. Have wisdom and ask for discernment whenever you use the Internet. I find that deception, broadly speaking, is increasing.

LUKE, JOHN, AND THE ACTS OF THE APOSTLES SHARE THEIR EXPERIENCE ON PENTECOST.

> Behold, I send the Promise of My Father upon you; but tarry in
> the city of Jerusalem until you are endued with power from on

high.

— LUKE 24:29

But the Advocate, the Holy Spirit, whom the Father will send in My name, will teach you all things and will remind you of everything I have told you.

— JOHN 14:26

And while they were gathered together, He commanded them: "Do not leave Jerusalem, but wait for the gift the Father promised, which you have heard Me discuss.

— ACTS 1:4

Jesus told them to wait. I don't believe they had any idea what they would receive. They all followed the Lord going to the Upper Room in Jerusalem.

This was the time of a solemn fast followed by a feast called Shavuot which marks the fifty days after Jesus' Resurrection from the dead.

Which is the earnest of our inheritance until the redemption of the purchased possession, unto the praise of his glory.

— EPHESIANS 1: 14

These brethren of Christ, still grieving the loss of the savior, had another thing to be concerned about. Some held much malice towards Christ and His followers of The Way. These one hundred and twenty people did not classify themselves as a religion but as believers of The Way. Unbeknownst to them, while they waited for what Jesus had promised; another was planning on hunting them down to shackle and deliver them to Roman authorities.

And Saul, yet breathing out threatening and slaughter against the disciples of the Lord, went unto the high priest, and desired of him letters to Damascus to the synagogues, that if he found any of this way, whether they were men or women, he might bring them bound unto Jerusalem.

And as he journeyed, he came near Damascus: and suddenly there shined round about him a light from heaven:

And he fell to the earth, and heard a voice saying unto him, Saul, Saul, why persecutest thou me?

And he said, Who art thou, Lord? And the Lord said, I am Jesus whom thou persecutest: it is hard for thee to kick against the pricks.

And he trembling and astonished said, Lord, what wilt thou have me to do? And the Lord said unto him, Arise, and go into the city, and it shall be told thee what thou must do.

And the men who journeyed with him stood speechless, hearing a voice, but seeing no man.

And Saul arose from the earth; and when his eyes were opened, he saw no man: but they led him by the hand, and brought him into Damascus.

And he was three days without sight, and neither did eat nor drink.

— ACTS 9: 1-2

And when the day of Pentecost was fully come, they were all with one accord in one place.

And suddenly there came a sound from heaven as of a rushing mighty wind, and it filled all the house where they were sitting.

And there appeared unto them cloven tongues like as of fire, and it sat upon each of them.

And they were all filled with the Holy Ghost and began to speak with other tongues, as the Spirit gave them utterance.

And there were dwelling at Jerusalem Jews, devout men, out of every nation under heaven.

Now when this was noised abroad, the multitude came together and were confounded, because every man heard them speak in his language.

And they were all amazed and marveled, saying one to another, Behold, are not all these which speak Galileans?

And how to hear we every man in our tongue, wherein we were born?

— ACTS 2:1-8

By Acts 13:9, Saul, the tormentor, is now Paul, the disciple following his conversion to Christianity. He begins his first writings in the Book of Acts.

There is one utterance of The Spirit known as tongues. And there is one of the Gifts of the Spirit to Discern tongues. You should expect to speak in tongues if you are sanctified and filled with the Spirit of God. It is your birthright. Jesus promised His followers to wait for the comforter whom He would send. Speaking in tongues is your spiritual language and is understood by heaven. I do not find it difficult to understand that while the Angels of God are most likely able to discern 7,100 languages of the earth, one spiritual language can fix many problems, not to mention it's not the enemy's native tongue. I sometimes know what's on my heart when I pray in tongues; at other times, I have no idea. I can pray for minutes, hours, or until I fall asleep. I feel accomplished after praying in tongues. I call it my Holy Rant, and there is a definite beginning and end when it happens.

There are few clues in the Bible about our greatest adversary. We need to start with Ezekiel Chapter 28; 1-28. This passage is from the Amplified Holy Bible.

> *The WORD of the LORD came again to me:*
> *"Son of man, say to the prince of Tyre, " Thus says*
> *   the Lord God:*
> *"Because your heart is lifted up*
> *   and you have said and thought, 'I am a god,*
> *I sit in the seats of the gods,*
> *   in the heart of the seas,'*
> *Yet you are (only) a man, weak and feeble, and*
> *   not God,*
> *   though you imagine yourself to be more than*
> *   mortal*
> *and think your mind is as wise as the mind of God.*
> *Behold you are imagining yourself wiser than*
> *   Daniel;*
> *There is no secret that you think is hidden*
> *   from you.*
> *With your (own) wisdom and your (own) under-*
> *   standing*
> *You have acquired your riches and power*
> *   you have brought gold and silver*
> *   into your treasuries;*
> *By Your great wisdom and by Your trade*
> *   you have increased your riches and power,*

And your heart is proud and arrogant because of
  your wealth—
Therefore says the LORD GOD,
Because you have imagined your mind (to be)
like the mind of God (Having thoughts and plans
  like God Himself),
Therefore, behold, I will bring strangers (Babyloni-
  ans) upon you
  The most ruthless and violent of the nations;
And they will draw their swords against the beauty
  of your wisdom
  and defile your splendor.
They will bring you down into the pit of destruction,
  And you shall die the death of all those that die
  in the heart of the seas.
Will you still say, 'I am a god,'
  in the presence of those who kill you?
But you are (only) a man, (made of earth) and
  not God.
  In the hands of those who wound and
  profane you
You will die the death of the uncircumcised
  (barbarian)
  By the hand of strangers, For I have spoken says
  the LORD God.

A Lament over the King of Tyre

Again the word of the Lord came to me saying:

Son of man, take up a dirge (funeral poem to be sung) for and say
to him, Thus says the Lord God the king of Tyre, and say to him,
Thus says the Lord God:

You had the full measure of perfection and the finishing touch (of completeness), Full of wisdom and perfect in beauty

full of wisdom and perfect in beauty.

You were in Eden, the garden of God;

every precious stone was your covering,

The ruby, the Topaz, and the diamond

The beryl, the onyx, and the jasper,

The lapis lazuli, the turquoise, and the emerald,

And the gold the workmanship of your of your settings and sockets, was in you.

They were prepared

On the day you were created

You were an anointed cherub, who covers and protects. And I placed you there.

you were on the holy mountain of God;

you walked amid the stones of fire (sparkling jewels) Ex 24:10

You were blameless in your ways

from the day you were created,

until unrighteousness and evil were found in you.

Through the abundance of your commerce

You were internally filled with lawlessness and you sinned;

Therefore I have cast you out as an unholy thing, From the mountain of God

and I have destroyed you,

From the midst of the stones of fire.

Your heart was proud and arrogant because of your beauty;

You destroyed your wisdom for the sake of your splendor.

I cast you to the ground;

I lay you before kings, That they might look at you

You profaned your sanctuaries; by the great quantities of your sins *and* the enormity of your guilt, by the unrighteousness of your trade

Therefore I have brought forth a fire from your midst, It has consumed you

And I have reduced you to ashes on the earth, In the sight of all who look at you.

All the peoples (nations) who knew you are appalled at you

are appalled at you; you have come to a horrible and terrifying end and all will forever cease to be.

— GENESIS 3:14 15: IS 14:12; MATT 16:31

You were in Eden, the garden of God;

every precious stone was your covering,

The ruby, the Topaz, and the diamond

The beryl, the onyx, and the jasper,

The lapis lazuli, the turquoise, and the emerald,

And the gold the workmanship of your of your settings and sockets, was in you.

They were prepared

On the day you were created

— EZEKIEL 28:13

God describes His creation through the prophet Ezekiel. God
created Angels to be a little lower than man (Hebrews 2:7). The
Angel made with the covering of precious stones was the Worship
angel with pipes, noted as setting and sockets, allowing the
creation of sounds. As the creation process commenced, this angel
was responsible for creative sound or music.

Sound has creative powers. The voice of God created the heavens
and the earth. Lucifer, the scripture says, has wisdom. He gets that
wisdom from walking on the hot stones of Revelation Knowledge
on the Holy Mountain of God.

His job was to walk among the hot stones of the fire and find revelations for the day, broadcasting them to the creation in the form of
music. This was in the very first days of creation. One can only
imagine the things that needed completion on day one to be ready
for the plan for day two.

Like an expediter, Lucifer expressed the new revelations as music
to the rest of God's world. One day, while in the hot stones, he saw
something concerning. It was a creation but not angelic, and he
found the idea of man. God had known the plan for man, and that
thought laid in the Revelation garden of hot stones; those plans to
create man, the bible tells, were to be used for day six. Before day
six, Lucifer could see that God created this man to be made higher
than the angels. Who was this competition GOD was thinking of?

You could say Lucifer was getting ahead of God, peeking in the stone garden to see what else he could see. We could call that disobedience in hindsight. People with more responsibility have more integrity required to be effective.

Can you see why the snake was in the Garden of Eden to affect mankind, which was now on earth with Adam, the first man, and Eve, the first woman?

Let us consider such a man as Job.

> And it was so when the days of their feasting were gone about, that Job sent and sanctified them, and rose early in the morning, and offered burnt offerings according to the number of them all: for Job said, It may be that my sons have sinned, and cursed God in their hearts. Thus did Job continually.
>
> Now there was a day when the sons of God came to present themselves before the Lord, and Satan came also among them.
>
> And the Lord said unto Satan, Whence comest thou? Then Satan answered the Lord, and said, From going to and fro in the earth, and from walking up and down in it.
>
> And the Lord said unto Satan, Hast thou considered my servant Job, that there is none like him in the earth, a perfect and an upright man, one that feareth God, and eschewed evil?
>
> Then Satan answered the Lord, and said, Doth Job fear God for nought?
>
> Hast, not thou made a hedge about him, and about his house, and about all that he hath on every side? thou hast blessed the work of his hands, and his substance is increased in the land.
>
> But put forth thine hand now, and touch all that he hath, and he will curse thee to thy face.

And the Lord said unto Satan, Behold, all that he hath is in thy power; only upon himself put not forth thine hand. So Satan went forth from the presence of the Lord.

And there was a day when his sons and his daughters were eating and drinking wine in their eldest brother's house:

And there came a messenger unto Job, and said, The oxen were plowing, and the asses feeding beside them:

And the Sabeans fell upon them, and took them away; yea, they have slain the servants with the edge of the sword; and I only am escaped alone to tell thee.

While he was yet speaking, there came also another, and said, The fire of God has fallen from heaven and hath burned up the sheep, and the servants, and consumed them, and I only am escaped alone to tell thee.

While he was yet speaking, there came also another, and said, The Chaldeans made out three bands, and fell upon the camels, and have carried them away, yea, and slain the servants with the edge of the sword; and I only am escaped alone to tell thee.

While he was yet speaking, there came also another, and said, Thy sons and thy daughters were eating and drinking wine in their eldest brother's house:

And, behold, there came a great wind from the wilderness: and smote the four corners of the house, and it fell upon the young men, and they are dead, and I only am escaped alone to tell thee.

Then Job arose, and rent his mantle, and shaved his head, and fell upon the ground, and worshipped.

And said, Naked came I out of my mother's womb, and naked shall I return thither: the Lord gave, and the Lord hath taken away; blessed be the name of the Lord.

In all this Job sinned not, nor charged God foolishly.

—JOB 5 5-22

And so Job died being old and full of days.

Satan did not win. God restored Job and he lived all the days written in his book.

—JOB 42:17

HAVE YOU BEEN TRIPPED UP IN THIS LIFE?

The thief cometh not but to steal and to kill and to destroy. I have come that they might have life and that they might have it more abundantly.

— JOHN 10:10

Abundance is the opposite of scarcity.

The Definition of Abundance: Having an ample quantity.

Where do you get your good vibes from? Your head or your surroundings? Neither answer is superior.

Where do you think the enemy will attack you, in your mind or surroundings? How does the enemy use your mind to trip you up?

Your imagination is one such way. Some people have more robust imaginations than others. It is best to ask God to check your imagination and offer His remedy if you are such a person. The enemy is persistent. More persistent than you could ever be.

If you have rouge thoughts flitting through your mind that involve lustful things, harmful things, I recommend you immediately ask God for His help.

> When Satan came to my bedside and told me to slit my wrists, I said not one word. When I opened my mouth to talk, I called out to Jesus.

> What am I talking about? It would be best if you did not converse with the enemy. How do I know this? When Lucifer was on the mountain tempting Jesus, and Satan said if you are The Son of God, make these rocks into bread, Jesus didn't have a discussion.

> — MATT 4:3

> Jesus said, "It is written: 'Man shall not live on bread alone, but on every word that comes from the mouth of God.'"

> — MATT 4:4

You can be oppressed by an evil spirit or possessed. You can pray to release oppression. Someone who has one or several spirits living on the inside will need deliverance. A minister of Jesus Christ who specializes in deliverance can help.

For oppression, Say this prayer every day upon waking and going to bed until you feel the oppression lift.

Pornography, infidelity, stealing, and other ill moral acts can sit on you, and the enemy can see it. He can hear your words; if he is in you, he may know you better than you know yourself.

Here is the prayer:

> *Lord Jesus Christ, I believe you are God's son and*
> *the only way to God. You died on the cross and*

*rose from the dead for my sins. I now confess all
sins and those you make known to me and the
sins of my ancestors. (Confess your sins out
loud one by one)*

*Lord, I repent of the sins I have ever committed. I
hate my sin; it sickens me, and I turn from all
my sins now. I thank you, Lord Jesus, for your
mercy and forgiveness, and thank you for your
love and blood that saves me. I renounce any
involvement with sin, remove it from me, and
forgive any person who has wronged me inten-
tionally or unintentionally, just as I ask you to
forgive me now.*

*I now claim your promise as my deliverance from
all evil and create in me a new person with your
holy spirit guiding me all my life.*

Amen

If a wicked thing has a hold on you, a diligent approach to be set free will be needed. I suggest daily communion until you feel the hold of sin has been lifted from you.

And He took bread, and gave thanks, and broke it, and gave it to them, saying, This is my body which is given for you; this do in remembrance of Me.

Likewise, also the cup after supper, saying, This cup is the New Testament in my blood which is shed for you.

— LUKE 22: 19-20

Whoever eats My flesh and drinks My blood remains in Me, and I in him.

— JOHN 6:56

It says in the Scripture Book that Moses and Elijah will return to earth after the rapture and during the tribulation to show people the way to Christ. As noted in Rev 11th Chapter.

Jude 9 Yet, Michael the Archangel when contending with the Devil disputed about the body of Moses, did not bring against him a railing accusation, but said The Lord rebukes You.

Imagine how Satan wanted to ruin the witness of Moses as noted in Rev 11.

I do believe just as Satan tried this stunt he is also working on humans of high stature in today's world to corrupt their thoughts and drive their actions to steal the testimony and land them in the pit.

I had an experience in the privacy of my bedroom when Satan tried to pull a fast one. I know he can be way more smooth than this. Know who you are talking to, ask for discernment

Plead the blood of Jesus over yourself and your children. Learn to repent quickly, Satan is on overdrive, He knows the time we are in better than most Christians.

> Then was Jesus led up of the Spirit into the wilderness to be tempted by the devil.
>
> And when he had fasted forty days and forty nights, he afterward hungered.
>
> And when the tempter came to him, he said, If thou be the Son of God, command that these stones be made bread.
>
> But he answered and said, It is written, Man shall not live by bread alone, but by every word that proceeded out of the mouth of God.
>
> — MATT 4; 1-4

A life not dedicated to God is a buffet table for Satan and his minions. It will happen slowly, and he tempts you; that is his first strategy. Tempt you to steal, think lustful thoughts, or those that don't honor life.

Once he sees you, don't resist that ploy; he will put that bull's eye on your back to notify the spiritual world of your fallen potential. Satan comes to seek, kill, and destroy, and Jesus died on the Cross for you so that you would have life and it more abundantly.

The choice is yours. You can submit to God or submit to the devil. One path leads to life, and the other to the smoky pit of eternal damnation. When God created Hell, He never intended for any man or woman to go there.

God in the Book of Genesis talked about the creation of man. God wanted a family. His first creation, Adam, was taken out by the serpent. Think of it: the Father of the human race, Adam, and the mother of the human race, Eve, are both disqualified for not obeying the rules provided by the Tree of the Knowledge of Good and Evil. God said to stay away. They were in constant communication with God. When I understood this close relationship, I had just gotten a new puppy, a spaniel. She stuck to me like glue in those early days. Sometimes, she would follow me into the bathroom or the garage, and I would come out and then go where's the dog? The dog was closed in the bathroom or the garage, wherever.

God was like this with Adam, who God said he could name the animals. God had big plans for Eve as well. When the honeymoon couple fell into sin after eating the apple, they hid from God.

Adam, where are you?

I have met people who are angry at God. These people have not read the bible, or maybe they have, and yet they are missing the point that Satan is the one who comes to seek, kill, and destroy. If

Satan can get you so mad at God that you turn away, that is a deal he can't refuse.

Please don't risk your future, your soul, or the blessings God has for you, which you have forfeited by blaming God for what Satan was responsible for. Instead, you are harboring unforgiveness, and that action is void of understanding Christ's power on the Cross.

What can you do? Ask God to help you. Ask for help if you are seeing the truth. State that you want to be set free from the binds that hold. And be freed by the death and the power of the resurrection of Christ, all done so that your sins are forgiven and forgotten.

Don't make it harder than it needs to be. God already knows what your sins are, and He truly loves you.

Once you are filled with the Spirit of God, you should speak in tongues. I was water-baptized when I began speaking in tongues. There are Christians amongst the Evangelicals who have the gift of seeding tongues, for lack of a better word.

> But you, beloved, building up yourselves on your most Holy Faith, praying I the Holy Spirit. (Our prayer thus being exercised in the realm of the Holy Spirit, motivates and empowered by Him.)
>
> — JUDE; 20

7

PLACES OF WORSHIP

If you want a church that believes in the fivefold ministry and the laying on of hands for healing, the Pentecostals follow this doctrine.

Many Baptist, Methodist, Catholic, and Lutheran churches give a Gospel message and follow the tenets of the Christian faith according to their denomination. The United Methodist Church has split, which is something to be aware of if you are looking for a church that follows scripture. The scripture-following group has moved away from the United Methodist denomination.

As I mentioned, I have been to churches across America as God has led. I look for certain things, and being ornate can be excluded. I love music, and a monthly Worship service that may go with a Tabernacle service is a good choice. On a typical worship day, a guitar or piano musician is lovely to provide worship ambiance.

I suggest you visit a few different churches in your area and find one that is suitable to God and your tastes. Here are a few examples of Churches where I have attended service.

- *A Small White Church*

I attended a Sunday service at a small white church in S. Carolina. The congregation was culturally mixed, had a busy nursery, and held three hundred parishioners.

Whenever I visit a church, I tithe a higher percentage than the customary ten percent.

This church posted the monthly tithing schedule in several places on the church property.

I like to have options, so this church piqued my curiosity, and I became anxious to give.

Monthly Tithing Schedule

Week 1-Missions

Week 2- Local Outreach and After-School Programs

Week 3- Self Directed

Week 4- Capital Fund

Week 5- Church Administration

I wrote separate checks for weeks 1, 2, and 5.

The sermon was targeted and powerful as to the responsibility to carry the gospel wherever God may take us. I remember thinking about the founding Fathers of America after hearing the word that Sunday.

- *A Small City Church*

I attended a small city church forty-five minutes away on a warm June day. I had met the church leader at a Leadership Conference, and she invited me to Sunday's service. I accepted the invitation.

The church was on a corner in a rough section of the city. Nevertheless, someone had taken the time to make the small sanctuary comfortable. There was a crucifix on the wall and a small statue of Christ in his customary robe and sandals. A wooden replica of the

Holy of Holies at the Tabernacle was on a side table. Light drapes on two windows allowed natural light into the sanctuary.

There were nine people in attendance, not including myself. As soft hymn music played as the final parishioners assembled, my mind wandered, imagining these city churches' heavy burden—working to impact their communities with the answer only the gospel can provide to bring change. I was also reminded of Jesus himself, who said people experiencing poverty will always have with them (Matt 26:11). My tithe was commensurate with the perceived need.

We sang several hymns; the church elder said a prayer of thanksgiving, and the Pastor read a verse out of Hebrews. A few church members had given testimonies of answered prayer. The Pastor said they had a modest and dedicated prayer team. The church body was invited to a small meal together at the church following the service.

The offering was then collected. I have a genuine heart for churches that do their best to put forth the gospel and follow the leadings of Christ. The offering was received, prayed over, and given thanks.

As we returned to our seats, the minister said this is the week we bless a church member each month by giving the service offering. I have never seen that scripture in the Bible. I was lost in my head again, with no scriptural reference to what I heard. Indeed, God would bless this effort. I was curious as to how the church found this biblical. I had my hunches. I heard joyous screaming at the altar as the recipient received the tithe amount. My mind was stuck on what I imagined was needed from my point of view.

Above all things, I am polite and remain to join in the delightful small meal shared with sweet believers.

It took me a while to understand what I had experienced. Sunday offerings are generally out of the public eye. However, this time, the process was transparent at the altar. I was the only shocked believer in the room that Sunday.

I have prayed for years for things that have yet to manifest. I believe strongly in the power of prayer. I know God's answer to prayer only needs to make sense to the person waiting for the manifest answer. I have also never been aware that I could actively participate in the answered prayer process. Honestly, that was the message for me on that beautiful June day.

- *A Palace for Christ in the Making*

I was on the East Coast, where a church was under new ownership, and restoration had begun.

People from the East, West, North, and South had come to lend their talents. I remember I couldn't imagine how Noah built that entire Ark.

In the first book, I talked about the people I met at this church. Everyone had a dream, saw a clue, or experienced some other leading that gave them the ability to go to the property and lend a hand.

The church's work teams adorned cloth drop sheets everywhere, with a sanctuary space for the parishioners. The nightly ministry provided no lack of powerful messages from seasoned ministers. Prophetic sessions and healing services were routinely available. Without a specific prayer but a word of knowledge in a hallway from Bob Jones, I came home with a confirmation of a word and a dream God had previously given me, and I no longer had Asthma or a nut allergy. Significant work was undoubtedly needed for the new ministry to take shape. I felt this was home for me.

Christ has called the church His body. We are to reach into all the earth with His Gospel. God did not call us to do Satellite ministry. Today's church must have open walls and a heart for the teachings of Christ. Outreach ministry is a must. Running a Christian School would be another choice. Regardless of the size of your church, mission support is crucial. It would be best if you also supported outreach. The two are not mutually exclusive.

I came home from that trip and stopped in the store to buy a can of mixed nuts. I had been allergic to nuts, which I first discovered at the age of two. Asthma also plagued me around the same age. I drove to the local hospital, pulled into the Emergency Department parking lot, and cracked open the can of nuts. The smell was inviting.

The remembrance sprang into my head, and I realized that we cannot please God without faith.

I drove ten minutes home, took the nuts out of the bag, and stood at the counter eating a walnut, a pecan, a cashew, and, lastly, a Brazil nut. The Brazil nut tingled my tongue a bit. Did you hear the man of God today say I could eat nuts? He did not single you out for any reason. I brushed my teeth and went to bed.

- *A Grand City Church on New Year's Eve*

I prayed about this church visit, but I received no word from God, so I went. I once lived in this city, and I knew this church's history. It began operating in 1827, and a revival ensued a few years later,

In 1827, church life was gone, and drinking and spending time in bars consumed the citizens. Charles Grandison Finney, with unique methods of evangelism, gained the title of "Father of modern revivalism."

His methods paved the way for evangelists like Dwight Moody, John Chapman, Billy Sunday, and Billy Graham.

The church was a classic. I could not feel the Spirit in the church and soon heard why.

The then Pastor gave a sermon on the universe, and he read a story, a child's story as I remember it, about the moon and wished everyone a Happy New Year. I drove home with a revival fire brewing in my belly as my prayer language kicked into high gear and the snowflakes swirled all around in my headlights.

You may invite other believers to your home for bible study and fellowship. There are online churches where you can hear a sermon as a group with a discussion time to follow. You may rent a room at your local library for a meeting place on a Saturday. Again, God will make way for you. All you need to do is ask and thank Him for helping you.

- *A South Eastern Church*

I arrived at this thousand-seat church God had instructed me to visit on a cool Autumn night. I can sense God and the Holy Spirit in many churches, and this one was no different. I had arrived early, as my flight had arrived early for a change.

I had a cup of coffee and a half sandwich packed for when needed. There were a few picnic tables in the back of the church, so I opened my Bible and sipped on the coffee. As I opened to the Psalms verse, my gaze was averted by four deer peeking through the treeline at me.

Oh Dear, I didn't think to bring apples, I said. They all shook their heads. I'll remember tomorrow, I promised. Just then, four people walked toward me, and the deer disappeared. The two couples were from Maryland. We talked about our hotels. We were lodging in adjacent hotels and decided to get a late bite if needed and able. More guests began arriving, and we decided to enter the sanctuary.

I went to the second row, and the outside left seat was open. There were Bibles on the held seats, and a few people were sitting in the long row. I quieted myself, thanking God for getting me here and asking for blessing on all people traveling to this location. A music track with a piano was playing softly. In another five minutes, the bright lights were switched to a mellow light. Many people entered the sanctuary, and those playing instruments ascended to the stage.

There were a few green plants at the altar, purple and gold drapes at the back of the altar, and a nearly life-size wooden cross stood in the back center stage. This told me I was in the place I expected to be—or, more to the point, the place God expected me to be.

The brochures circulated, as there were several guest speakers, and an intermission would be called if approved. This meant if the Holy Spirit said take a break. I had never been to a church service God sent me to where an intermission was called, so I wasn't expecting one. I took a few bites of my sandwich and a few swigs of coffee. I don't wear my watch to church service. The band struck their first cord, the house was packed, and here we go.

Praise and Worship sprang to life, and a minister came to the podium. Some parishioners had gone up front to the altar. The music was lovely, with three musicians and a pianist. The lights dropped over the worshipers, and the lights on the altar were now softly lit.

After fifty minutes, the minister thanked the musicians as they parted the stage, said a prayer, and thanked God for all in attendance. The minister preached on the first church and the Apostolic period up to 100 AD. The Cross must not fall from the American church. Did we know God was sending Angels to earth not to measure sin but to measure the church? Yes, I believed that.

The minister continued to preach about the church's role today being different from any time before. The time we live in makes that a reality.

I was looking at the altar, and the minister's voice was present, but I sat puzzled by the sight before me. I could see a rugged path to the round building ahead. I followed the path and noticed the door was slightly ajar, so I peeked through the crack. On a podium sat an Angel in brilliant white clothing and golden shoes, and I knew he was an Angel waiting on a reassignment. He had been waiting a long time and was okay, just as he was.

I snapped to the people next to me were switching seats. Are you moving I asked the woman. Oh no, the man next to my husband said he has to talk to you about something, We'll be right back. I don't know anyone here, or I shouldn't know anyone. What is this about I wondered.

The man sat down where the woman had been, he had beautiful eyes.

Did you see it? He asked.

See what?

The building.

(I had never had this happen to me before, of which I was aware, where another person saw the same vision I saw.)

This is strange.

So, did you see it?

Do you mean the round building? I asked.

Yes, did you see what was inside?

I peeked inside and saw a beautiful angel waiting for a reassignment.

Gold shoes?

Yes.

I asked God who the angel was, and He asked me to ask you.

You're kidding me.

No, who is the Angel?

He was AJ Tomlison's angel.

I marveled that my own child had AJ initials.

This preacher preached to the Native people and I believe God will be bringing those souls into the modern church movement in these last days.

The man patted me on my right thigh, and his eyes blazed excitedly.

You're good, he said as he returned to his seat, and the woman sitting next to me returned to her seat.

We had no intermission, and it was only 11:30 p.m. Thankfully, I found my way back to my hotel and didn't see the people who wanted to grab a bite, and I needed sleep more than I needed food.

I brushed my teeth and lay in bed. It all happened so fast that I didn't even know the man's name.

I asked God what do you want me to know about what happened in that church service tonight? Something like this has never happened to me before, and it put me on high alert.

The Spirit's voice said It was the first time for both of you. The Spirit said this was how the church would operate in the next season. The ministry of Jesus is the guide. I asked for more information.

The Pastor is to live in the prayer closet. The lay people of the church are not lay people. They are disciples. Disciples were the Administration of Christ. The Spirit voiced that your experience tonight confirms what I speak about.

So, more people will have this kind of experience of having others share the same visions they receive.

The Spirit voiced that many of God's children are experiencing this type of event to further the knowledge and ministry of Christ.

My mind began to race as I imagined the broader application of this shared process—certainly in witnessing and running a church, a soup kitchen, a nursery, a business, and so on.

I prayed, thanking God for helping me understand the process's very practical application. I needed to get to sleep, be up in time, go grocery shopping, and get some apples before church at 10 a.m.

You may have a small group of friends who believe in God and what Jesus did on the Cross. You may invite a group to your home for fellowship and Bible study. There are online churches that provide sermons that may be used in a home setting. Opening a question-and-answer time following can be aided with the use of a Repository Study Bible, which offers expanded teaching.

You can find many types of study guides online, such as free downloads or for a nominal fee.

When you study the Bible, you can start anywhere.

Begin by saying a simple prayer; God, I thank You for Your words in this Holy Bible so that I may draw closer to You as I read. I ask that my time of Bible study be made clear to me: Your desire as I honor You, Jesus. Amen.

The fourth chapter lists all the disciples, many of whom were in Jesus's presence. You could use this information to write short biographies of these believers. You can start by reading the words from the gospels written by each disciple. I started in Luke. I found that gospel to be very clear and concise. Write key points of interest. I use the study aids from The Daily Grace Company, an online store for reasonably priced study tools.

Listening to scriptures on tape can help you understand. The more you hear scripture, the more you learn. Share what you have learned with others and get clarification on areas as needed.

For a long time, when I needed a word from God, I opened the Bible, knowing that somewhere on those two pages, my answer lay.

I was watching a heartbreaking video the other day. In it, a pastor was being chastised by God for the unseen Sin he was carrying in his life, and he was sharing his discovery with his church body, which loved him.

You could hear the body of his church saying they didn't believe it. This could not be, but the Pastor pressed on.

He said he knew what God was saying but needed more information, and he was pleading with God to make himself clear. This Pastor said, "And I opened my Bible, just opened it, and whatever pages fall open, my answer is within."

There it was in stark detail. This Pastor's unconscious Sin manifested in the Holy Book's words. The Pastor was shocked, and he didn't fight God. He accepted the verdict and repented in front of his congregation. He is a faithful follower of Christ and a worthy leader. I expect his church to march valiantly into the harvest with his leadership.

This Christian life is not a competition, and we mustn't judge those who trip and stumble; instead, we must pray and support those who do their best with their lives dedicated to Christ and His teaching.

8

WHEN HEAVEN AND NATURE SING

The title of this Chapter, Heaven and Nature Sings, is something to think about. Nature may be beating us to the punch, singing to Heaven.

I love nature, and nothing surrounds me more thoroughly, as if I am alone with Christ, than when I am with His creation.

When I moved to the edge of the country, I knew I would encounter more animals. A boy from the neighborhood came down one day on New Year's telling me that when he drove home from the south end of the street heading north on the night before, it was snowing with a melody, and there were two deer on every front lawn down the street after midnight. He was amazed by what he saw. He said it was like a Christmas card, and everyone slept through it.

A week later, I was out beyond the fenced area. I saw the back sensor light kick on. I knew I had company, but I needed to figure out who. I was thinking of a cat or raccoon. It was a ten-point buck with girlfriends, and they all seemed to be talking as the snowflakes fell. He then turned, noticing me. We stood and admired each other as he took a step closer.

Was he asking if I was the one responsible for the apples in the snow last week and the week before? Bingo, I said as they ambled off.

Last spring, I had a mother Robin, nesting in my evergreen area near the side porch. I was first aware of her presence when I was weeding my flower garden off the side porch. We had a wind storm the night before, and while the sky was blue without a cloud, tree limbs and such were scattered. It was two o'clock in the afternoon when I got to weed-pulling.

I was focused on unwelcome weeds when I noticed two very blue eggs on the red mulch. Where did these eggs come from? I continued pulling weeds, thinking about the impossibility of those two eggs flying through the air from the tall trees along the driveway, making a soft landing in my garden.

I knew foxes, deer, and even squirrels would raid Robins' nests for eggs given the chance. All of those creatures frequented my property. I realized there was a dilemma with it being so late in the day. Then, out of nowhere, the mother bird flew out of an evergreen with a racket reminiscent of Alfred Hickocks' The Birds movie.

I darted to my porch and was in a quandary of what to do if anything. I was concerned about Mother Robin's nest at nightfall. A roaming four-legged creature could find those eggs in the garden and her nest.

The eggs lay in the blazing sun all afternoon. I knew she would destroy the eggs once she hatched her brood. How long would that take? I have never been to a funeral without flowers. I cut down the last few lilac sprigs. A few purple Alum slightly spent on strong stems and a tree branch with broad leaves. I laid the greenery on the air condition unit at the back of the garden and near the evergreen with the nest. Upon completion, it had a Hawaiian ambiance.

I had a beautiful white jar that once held expensive face cream. How did I know to save that jar? I had some soft pink netting, a few pieces of off-white velveteen scraps, and a pale pink satin square; the jar would be suitable.

With gloves on, I gently picked up the lovely blue eggs, one at a time, and laid them in the fabric-laced casket. I set the jar on the floral arrangement on the air conditioner's top. Dusk quickly set in, and the temperature began to drop as the sun faded. I wanted the mother to see her eggs. She flew above, looking down, and then landed on the air conditioner and stood quietly. Then she flew off.

I had a beautiful ribbon piece with trees and birdhouses on it. I walked to the backyard, where I had dug a big hole in one of the berms. I held the jar high above my head so Mother Bird could see her blue eggs as she flew above me. Stopping at the berm, I screwed the silver lid onto the jar and tied the ribbon snuggly around it. I placed the jar in the brown earth and shoveled soft soil over the snug top.

The rear yard sensor kicked on. I hoped she would get some sleep; it was a traumatic day for us both.

The next day, I stepped out to put the trash out, and she flew from her nest at my side door. We almost collided as she screamed her head off at me. I could only imagine the gist of her bird language. She didn't sleep after all.

I then activated my car door lock before I exited the house to give her time to adjust—a warning shot if you will. That worked out brilliantly. I put a bird bath in the garden and an open bird feeder further down the garden, away from her nest. I realized she didn't need any of this paraphernalia. Her prime objective was the tree line along the driveway and the stockade fence.

I knew this current mate could have been better at nest building. No judgment.

The only reward for the slight inconvenience was witnessing the first day of flight training inconvenience. What a joy to behold as those nearly grown Robins hung onto windowsills and made near-crash landings as the breeze tossed tree limbs.

Several days later, Mother Robin danced at the porch doorstep. I knew she was heading out as Dad continued to train the young. I congratulated her on a great job and said take good care, Momma. The month of May was moving in full swing.

In June, I was sitting on the porch and saw a fat Robin looking around from the top of the air-conditioned. Could it be Momma? Indeed, it was, and this time, she brought a five-star nest builder with her.

The weather had yet to warm up, and scant nest-building material was lying around. I had white shredded paper pieces and some short-course twine pieces. I laid those at the gardens egged. Those disappeared in moments. I emptied and cut tea bags into strips and put out more shredded paper. Before dinner, a suitable nest seemed done. Momma was very independent; she went for her worms despite the five-star builders offering. I missed that entire process due to work. I spied Momma on the stockade fence directly off the porch one day. She could not help but puff up. Another fine job, I told her as she swooped my way and flew away.

It was spring again. Time does fly. I came in from work, and there she was—fat Momma sitting in the bird bath, which held no water. The father, Robin, was high in the tree along the driveway. He didn't have to build a nest. The five-star nest held up through winter.

It was warmer this spring, and I was between jobs. I marked the calendar and had the brood due in three weeks. It was a slow three weeks. Then, all of a sudden, one day, I heard loud bird sounds. This was a hungry group. I could listen to their hunger pains. By afternoon, they were all three in the driveway chasing the chipmunk. I had purchased some mealworm food and placed some in the feeder and on the garden's edge.

It was dry, and we hadn't had much rain. Father Robin was working hard for the worms he was bringing back to the family. Mother Robin came onto the porch, and I knew she was taking off. I told her this last guy was a keeper. Good housebuilders are great, but a real family man is hard to find. She danced in a circle, and off she flew.

This father and his kids stayed longer than any brood because of the dry conditions. I cleaned and filled the bird bath daily and threw water down into the patches of lightly weed-filled spots to encourage earthworm movement. I had a new bag of mealy worm food that the kids were enjoying. I noted that in every Robin brood, there is one bird who is hungrier than the rest; this was true with cardinals also. I was very liberal with birdseed, and everyone else enjoyed it.

These young ones went after squirrels and chipmunks with ferocity like I hadn't seen before. I would pull into the driveway a few times and know a flutter all around, trying to avoid Robins in flight. As I parked the car, the chipmunk dashed under the car for cover.

Then, one day, the father and kids were gone...to where I didn't know, but I was sure worming and nest building was in the lesson plan. I was upstairs, and I heard a scream like I never had. I came downstairs to see one of the young Robins fly out of the nest, sit on the fence, and scream. I knew he must be hungry. I got the bird food and a few berries from the fridge and layered the outer edge of the garden with seeds and berries. Thankfully, the chipmunk and squirrel missed it.

The three Robins ate with delight, and off they went. I was sitting on the porch and saw Dad swooping in with more worms than he could almost carry. He went into the nest and popped back out. Oh dear, so sorry, I fed them. Dad flew up high into the tree and called out three times. I am not certain what he said, but in under two minutes, all those kids were back in the nest. I then pronounced him Father of the Year.

9

TESTIMONIES

I have watched World Data since becoming a nurse. World birth and death rates remained stable from 2015- 2019. The death rate rounded to 57 million globally rising to 63 million in 2019 and rising to 69 million in 2020. There is no data for 2022 or let's say date was available and is no longer. The death rate in 2023 was 60 million and the World-O-Meter app shows there have been 8 million global deaths in the first 7 weeks of the New Year of 2024.

I have confessed I never wanted to be a nurse. I had come out of a serious illness, and God provided a nursing scholarship and I took it. I knew a thing or two about medicine I had been a patient. I had twenty nurses taking care of me and six of them were my favorites. If I was going to be a nurse I too would take excellent care of my patients. I moaned and groaned for a few years. I will tell you facing death and then living to remember it, that can have strange effects on someone. Then one day out of the blue it hit me, I was one of the luckiest people alive. I tell you this because if you have been through a physical trial or the person you love has been, be patient, this too shall pass.

I have never left my body. I was in Heaven in a vision. I was in a Wedding Hall as noted in my first book. This claimant had been badly injured. He had slipped into and out of life like loose jelly.

He thought he was in Central Park in New York City and although the huge Angel at his side informed him he was no longer on earth without saying a word.

As he and the Angel walked down the path or a manicured pathway, he noted the noise as he moved along. I have had some patients tell me heaven is noisy. The place was humming with joy. He could see the Park, the area to his left just ahead, and the river to his right. Big trees dipped in and were drinking for the river and without words the Angel told him it was the river of life.

Tall trees like Sycamores were arraigned in a perfect circle inside the fenced enclosure. Then he noticed angels, flames of light flying into and out from behind the trees. There was a rainbow in the sky beyond the trees. Notable was a low humming sound from beyond the trees and some flashes of light.

The man's guardian angel told him he was pleased today's trip could be made manifest. The Angel described the actions that were not visible from where the man stood. The park-like area is Command Central where sits the Throne of God Almighty. The activity seen now is the happening of the answering of prayer. The answering of prayer is not just the decision of God the Father; but rather a committee process to find the best answer.

I almost could not believe what I was hearing. I had heard of people getting answers to prayer that were better than their expected outcome. I was concerned because I had several prayers on the line with a sincerely held expected response.

I was hoping my answered prayer wasn't a committee answer, that's just me. I am beyond thankful that God cares for me and if

He knows better than I, how a situation should turn out, well praise God for the answer.

I have prayed for many things. I have received many things from God for which I never prayed. God always told me about it, sometimes after the fact that indeed it was from Him. And my obedience was somehow involved.

Imagine a busy regional airport, small jets flying in and out at a rapid clip. The Angels are the aircraft from Heaven to Earth and Earth to Heaven maybe to a lesser degree these angels pull in with clues, seen testimony, things they saw written in a believer journal, requests, heartaches, and hot off-the-press prayers. Angels flying out have answers, maybe dreams, prophetic words, or even hunch for the believer. The possibilities are endless and The Guardian Angel explained that the answer was a very well-researched topic before the agreed-upon answer was dispatched.

The man heard signing at the Throne Room of God, Holy, Holy, Holy, as the angels of God commenced in their mission of receiving and answering prayer.

I do sing to Heaven and God with my words. Sometimes my spiritual language and other times I use this verse;

You are my God, you are my Lord, you are the Christ, and you are the Son, the moon the stars. It is your face of beauty, your heart of love, a righteousness that clothes you well and you are mine, my lovely Lord, and your cross is the passion for all. Holiness clothes you and this I adore, guide me, and teach forever more.

I say in all honesty I have always believed in Heaven. I believed because the Bible told me so. There are things in the Bible story that I believe without a doubt. The Bible is believable. Do you have any idea how very much God loves you? He does not love as a man loves. He loves with a love so warm and forgiving that asking for forgiveness is the first place to start no matter how far away from Him you think you are.

I am thankful for the great care that was taken to get all the Spirit-inspired words from all the saints into the Holy Book.

My patient who I had not yet met was severely hurt. I cried when I read his surgical trauma report. As I sat staring at the surreal report I realized he checked out and back in a few times. Oh glory he took a trip, I'd bet my paycheck on it. It is a tender ordeal even years after the fact. One day at lunch I asked him. Did he go anywhere on that fate full day?

He did. I love this story because I know he will be healed and he is ever so patient.

He found himself in a huge movie theater. He was sitting in the seat and suddenly his best friend from high school came into the theater to see him. His friend had heard he had arrived. My client said his friend had passed several years ago. He still knew his mother and he said he knew he must tell his friend's mother that her son was in heaven. Just then a movie trailer started playing and it was all his family members in the film. None of his immediate family had left Earth. He was curious why that happened. God was reminding him he had family still earthbound. He tried to follow his friend as he left the theater and his friend started running away and he lost him.

This is a lovely story of the grace of God. This man had been through enough and landing in a waiting room in heaven was a very decent thing.

10

THE FINAL CHAPTER

The Bible is amazing. A Who- Done- It kind of book. The people in the Old Testament saw things they probably didn't know how they fit in their present day as they called for Christ hundreds of years before His birth on earth. The Jewish people who knew the Torah well and were in a very large part dependent on God also missed Christ's arrival to earth.

Daniel saw visions that speak of passages in Revelations.

The book of Daniel opens with the First Deportation of the Israelites to Babylon by King Nebuchadnezzar and Daniel and his friend are chosen for the King's service.

And the king spoke unto Ashpenaz the master of his eunuch, that he should bring certain of the Children of Israel, and of the King's seed and the princes.

Children who have no blemish, but are well-favored, and skillful in all wisdom, and cunning in knowledge, and understanding science and such as had ability in them to stand in the Kind's palace, and whom they might teach the learning of the tongue of the

Chaldeans. (Scholars believe this is skill with the Aramaic language and writing employed by ancient Babylon)

And the king appointed them a daily provision of the king's meat, and of the wine which he drank: so nourishing for three years, that at the end thereof they might stand before the king.

Now among these were the children of Judah, Daniel, Hananiah, Mishael, and Azariah.

Their Names are ordered to be changed by the king Nebuchadnezzar

> Unto whom the prince of the eunuchs gave names; for he gave unto Daniel the name Belteshazzar, and to Hananiah, of Shadrach: and to Mishael of Meshach; and Azariah of Abed-Nego.
>
> By changing their names Nebuchadnezzar was trying to blot out the names and memory of Jehovah, the God of the Hebrews.
>
> But Daniel purposed in his heart that he would not defile himself with the portion of the king's meat, nor with the wine he drank; therefore he requested of the prince of the eunuchs that he might not defile himself.
>
> Now God had brought Daniel in favor and tender love with the prince of the eunuchs.
>
> — BOOK OF DANIEL 1: 3-9

As a believer, you know the story of Daniel and his two friends, as they are tossed into the fire with four people seen in the furnace, by the king with no ill effect. Daniel is sent to the lion pit to be devoured and God closes shut the mouths of the lions. Daniel solidifies himself as a man of God not to be changed by a king's decree.

Daniel Chapter Two: Nebuchadnezzar's Dream Calls His Wise Mean

Then the king commanded to call the magicians, the astrologers, the sorcerers, and the Chaldeans to show the king his dreams, so they came and stood before the king.

Nebuchadnezzar Demands this cast of characters to recall his dream for him.

But if you show me the dream, and the interpretation thereof; you shall receive of me gifts and rewards and great honor.

They answered again and said, Let the king tell his servants the dream, and we will show the interpretation of it.

The Chaldeans answered before the king, and said, There is not a Man upon the Earth who can shew the king matter therefore there is no king, lord not ruler who asked such a thing at any magician, or astrologer or Chaldean.

For this cause, the king was furious and commanded to destroy all the wise men of Babylon.

And the decree went forth that the wise men should be slain, and they sought Daniel and his fellows to be slain.

The Dream was revealed to Daniel

Thou O king saw and behold a great image, This great image, whose brightness was excellent, stood before you, and the form thereof was terrible.

This image's head was of fine gold, his breast and his arms of silver, his belly and his thighs of brass

His leg is of iron, his feet part of iron and clay.

Then was the iron, the clay, the brass, the silver, and the gold broken to pieces together and became like the chaff of the summer threshing floors; and the wind carried them away, that no place was found for them and the stone that smote the image became a great mountain and filled the whole earth.

> *2:36 This is the dream, and we will tell the interpretation thereof before the king.*
> Head of Gold is Babylon
> Breast and Arms of Silver; Medo-Persia
> Belly and thighs of Brass; Grecia (Grecian Empire which proclaims the rise of Alexander the Great)
> Legs of Iron; Rome The Romain Empire the Strongest of all.
> Feet of Iron and Clay; Revised Roman Empire of current day
> *A Klas Swab is talking about putting chips (Metal) into (Adam was formed from clay before God breathed life into him) humans, this is what Daniel saw as he counseled Nebuchadnezzar about the dream he had.*
> *2:41 And whereas you saw the feet and toes, part of the potters' clay, and part of the iron, the kingdom shall be divided; but there shall be in it of the strength of iron for as much as you saw iron mixed with miry clay.*
> *2:42 And as the toes of the feet were part of iron, and part of clay, so the kingdom shall be partly strong and partly broken.*

As we read the Book of Revelations as seen by John as we talk about the horse riders with power nowhere is it stated that God provided power to the horse riders. We can look and determine with some prayer and bible study where we are in the timeline today knowing that no one except the Father knows the day or the time that will be as a blink of an eye known as the Rapture of the Body of Christ. Believe no man who says Rapture is this date. Even Christ does not know, only the Father.

The Book of Revelation

You will perhaps understand a historical fact better if you have some knowledge of world history. It is a Known fact that famines can be produced by many factors and the act of war holds the top spot for famine after a war. The first seal has scholars suggesting Alexander the Great date thumbnail. I would suggest you pray for wisdom, some people get understanding in dreams which often need some deciphering. However you work to fact find is a good practice knowing no one knows the day or the hour of the first spiritual happening that plucks earth dwellers to safety.

Revelation Chapter Six

First Seal

6:1 And I saw when the Lamb opened one of the
Seals and I heard, as it were the noise of thun-
der, one of the four beasts saying Come and see

6:2 And I saw behold a white horse and he who sat
on him had a bow and a crown was given unto
him, and he went forth conquering and to
conquer.

6:3 And when He had opened the **second Seal**, *I*
heard the second beast say, Come See.

6:4 And there went out another red horse and
power was given unto him who sat thereon to
take peace from the earth, and that should kill
one another; and there was given to him a great
sword.

6:5 And then when He had opened the **third a Seal**,
I heard a third beast say, Come and see. And I

beheld, and lo a black horse and he who sat on him had a pair of balances in his hand.

*6:7 And when He had opened the **fourth Seal**, I heard the voice of the fourth beast say. Come and See.*

6:8 And I looked and behold s pale horse and his name that sat on him was Death, and Hell followed with him. And power was given unto them over the fourth part of the earth, to kill with the sword, and with hunger, and with death, and with the beasts of the earth.

*6:9 And when He had opened the **fifth Seal**, I saw under the Alter the souls of those who were slain for the Word of God, and for their testimony which they held. (See Rev 2;11).*

6:10 They cried with a loud voice saying, How Long, O Lord, Holy, and True, do you not judge and avenge our blood on them who dwell in the earth?

6:11 And white robes were given unto every one of them; and it was said unto them that they should rest yet for a little season until their fellow servants also and their brethren, who should be killed as they were should be fulfilled.

*6:12 And I beheld when He had opened the **sixth Seal** and lo, there was a great earthquake; and the sun became black as sackcloth of hair, and the moon became as blood.*

6:13 And the stars of heaven fell unto the earth, even as the fig tree casts her untimely figs when she is shaken of a mighty wind.

6:14 And the Heaven departed as a scroll when it is rolled up and every mountain and island were moved out of their places.

*6:15 And the kings of the earth, and the great men,
and the rich men, and the chief captains, and
the mighty men, hid themselves in the dens in
the rocks of the mountains*

*6:16 And said to the rocks and the mountains Fall
on us, and hide us from the face of Him Who sits
on the Throne, and from the wrath of the Lamb.*

6:17 For the great day of his wrath has come.

Revelation Chapter Seven

*7:1 And after these things I saw four Angels
standing on the four corners of the earth,
holding the four winds of the earth, that the
wind should not blow on the earth, nor the sea,
nor any tree.*

*7:2 And I saw another Angel ascending from the
east, having the Seal of the Living God, and he
cried with a loud voice to the four Angels, to
whom it was given to hurt the earth and the sea*

*7:3 Saying hurt not the earth, neither the sea nor
trees till we have sealed the servants of our God
in their foreheads.*

*7:4 And I heard the numbers of them which were
sealed. And there were a hundred forty and four
thousand of all the Tribes of the Children of
Israel.*

*7:5 Of the Tribe of Judah were sealed twelve thou-
sand, Of the Tribe of Reuben were sealed twelve
thousand*

*7:6 Of the Tribe of Asher were sealed twelve thou-
sand. Of the Tribe of Nephthalim were sealed
twelve thousand. Of the Tribe of Manasses were
sealed twelve thousand.*

7:7 Of the Tribe of Simeon were sealed twelve thou-

sand. Of the tribe of Levi were sealed twelve thousand.

7:8 Of the Tribe of Zabulon were sealed twelve thousand. Of the Tribe of Joseph were sealed twelve thousand. Of the Tribe of Benjamin were sealed twelve thousand.

7:9 After this I beheld, and, lo a great multitude, which no man could number, of all nations, and kindreds, and people, and tongues, stood before the Throne, and before the Lamb clothed in white robes, and palms in their hands. (These are the martyrs who gave up their lives for The Lord Christ in the great Tribulation.)

7:10 And cried with a loud voice saying Salvation to our God which sits upon the Throne and unto the Lamb.

Revelation Chapter Eight

8:1 And when He had opened the seventh Seal, there was silence in Heaven in about the space of one-half hour.

It is important to note that the heavens had gone quiet only one other time and that was before the great floods in the days of Noah.

8:2 And I saw the seven Angels who stood before God, and to them were given seven Trumpets.

8:3 And another Angel came and stood at the Alter, having a Golden Censer, that He should offer it with all the prayers of all the Saints upon the Golden Alter which was before the throne.

8;4 And the smoke of the Incense, which came with the prayers of the Saints ascended before God out of the Angel's hand.

*8:5 And the Angel took the censer and filled it with
the fire of the alter and cast it onto the earth,
And there were voices and thundering, and light-
ning and an earthquake.
8:6 And the Seven Angels which had the Seven
Trumpets prepared themselves to sound.*

First Trumpet

*8:7 The First Angel sounded, and therefore followed
Hail and fire mingled with blood, and they have
cast upon the earth and a third part of the trees
was burnt up.*

Second Trumpet

*8:8 And the second Angel sounded, and as it were a
great mountain burning with fire; was cast into
the sea; and a third part of the sea became
blood.
8:9 And a third part of the creatures which were in
the sea, and had life died; which were in the sea
and the third of the ships were destroyed.*

Third Trumpet

*8:10 And the third Angel sounded, and there was a
great Star from heaven burning as if it was a
lamp, and it fell on a third of a part of the
rivers, and upon the fountains of water.
8:11 And the name of the Star was Wormwood and
the third part of the waters became wormwood
and many men died of the waters because they
were made bitter.*

The Fourth Trumpet

8:12 And the fourth Angel sounded and a third of

the sun was smitten, and the third part of the moon and the third part of the stars; so as the third part of them was darkened, the day shone not for a third part of it and the night likewise.

8:13 And I beheld and heard an Angel flying through the midst Heaven, saying with a loud voice; Woe, woe, woe to the inhabitants of the earth because of the other voices of the Trumpet of the three Angels which are yet to sound.

The Fifth Trumpet

9:1 And the fifth Angel sounded, and I saw a star fall from Heaven unto the earth, and to him was given the key to the bottomless pit.

9:2 And he opened up the bottomless pit, and there arose a smoke out of the pit, as the smoke of a great furnace, and the sun and the air were darkened because of the smoke of the pit.

9:3 And there came out of the smoke locusts upon the earth, and unto them was given power, as scorpions of the earth have power.

9:4 And it was commanded them that they did not hurt the grass of the earth, neither any green thing, neither any tree, but only those men which have not the seal of God in their forehead.

This is not a scare tactic; it is the closest thing to the future truth known to man.

YOUR PRAYER OF SALVATION

Dear Father God,

I need you more today than any other day. I sincerely apologize that I turned my back on you until now. I am told you are full of grace and mercy and I fall at the foot of your cross to ask for forgiveness and receive it with gladness and thanksgiving.

I believe in your Son Jesus and the Cross where he gave His life for me and I repent from my sins and I live only for you and your purpose for my life. Have your way with me and create in me a clean heart Oh, God.

Amen